SOWING SEEDS OF GENEROSITY

Jean-Eric Duval
Sowing Seeds of Generosity
Shaping Lives, Changing Destinies

Published by Spines
ISBN: 979-8-89691-124-1

SOWING SEEDS OF GENEROSITY

CHANGING LIVES, SHAPING DESTINIES

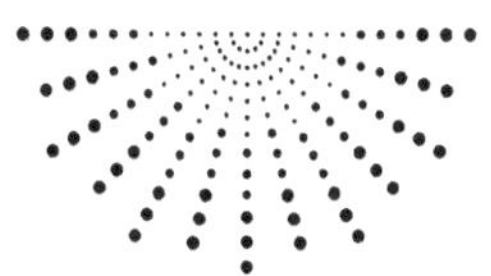

JEAN-ERIC DUVAL

CONTENTS

ABOUT THE AUTHOR

Presentation of the author of the book "Sowing Seeds of Generosity: Changing Lives, Shaping Destinies."

Jean Éric Duval, the author of this inspiring book, is a recognized educator and leader with more than 20 years of experience in teaching physical education and managing educational programs. Holding two master's degrees, one in Leadership and Development at the Northern Christian University of Haiti (UCNH) and the other in Science and Development at the State University of Haiti, Jean Éric has dedicated his career to training, mentoring, and motivating young people and professionals through various educational programs.

Throughout his career, he has held several positions of responsibility, notably as a teacher, program coordinator, and project manager in international organizations such as Catholic Relief Services and Finn Church Aid. His passion for teaching and his commitment to community development are reflected in his ability to lead teams, organize events, sports, and promote personal growth among his students and colleagues.

With his international experience, Jean Éric is also trilingual (English, Creole, and French), which allows him to expand his influence and bring his expertise into multicultural contexts. Today, he shares his vision and experiences through his literary work, encouraging everyone to sow seeds of generosity in the lives of others.

PREFACE

It is with great joy and deep humility that I write this foreword for a book as inspiring as *Sowing Seeds of Generosity: Shaping Lives, Changing Destinies.* Through these pages, the author takes us on a spiritual and human journey, highlighting the strength and beauty of generosity, not only as an act but as a true vocation.

In a world where individualism and selfishness often seem to prevail, this book reminds us that generosity is much more than a simple act of kindness. It is the reflection of God's love through our lives and actions. Every gift, every act of compassion, every moment dedicated to others becomes a precious seed, planted in hearts and meant to produce abundant fruit.

The author has managed, with wisdom and depth, to demonstrate to us that giving is not limited to material goods. Sharing our time, our love, our listening, and our attention has a lasting impact on those around us. It is thus that we are called to emulate Jesus Christ, the greatest example of generosity.

I highly recommend this book to all those who wish to be instruments of peace and blessing in the lives of others. May this book be a source of inspiration and motivation for you, urging you to sow generosity every day with love and faith.

Rev. Dr. Jean Bilda Robert
President of the UEBH and National Director of the International Bible League-Haiti

ACKNOWLEDGMENTS

First of all, I give glory to God, the supreme giver, for His infinite grace and unmerited blessings. Without Him, nothing we achieve would make sense. It is through His benevolent hand that I have reached this precious moment in my life, celebrating 52 years under His protection and divine guidance.

To my family, my pillar and constant support, I express my deep gratitude. To Wilnouse, my wonderful wife, and to our children, Jemima and Christoffer, thank you for your unconditional love, your patience, and your unwavering support. You are the quiet strength behind every step of this journey.

I also wish to thank all the benefactors who made this Thanksgiving celebration possible. Your generosity has sown an abundance of blessings in my life. May God repay you a hundredfold for what you have so freely given. To my friend from Georgia, Rachelle, thank you for that simple call that stirred deep reflection within me, and served as the catalyst for this beautiful spiritual and fraternal adventure. Your gesture reminded me of the importance of sowing in the lives of others.

To all those who participated in the Thanksgiving evening for my 52nd birthday, your prayers, your presence, and your acts of kindness made this celebration unforgettable. You have sown in my life and in the lives of those present that evening, and I am convinced that these seeds will bear abundant fruit.

Finally, this book, "Sowing Seeds of Generosity: Shaping Lives, Changing Destinies", is the living testimony of what we can accomplish together, when we choose to sow with love and faith. May this book be a source of inspiration for each of you, so that you too can sow in the lives of those around you.

Thank you all, may God bless you abundantly.

SUMMARY

This book delves into the transformative power of generosity as an act of faith and love towards others. Jean-Eric Duval uses biblical examples and personal testimonies to demonstrate how generosity can enrich both the giver and the receiver spiritually and materially. Inspired by figures like the widow of Zarephath, Zacchaeus, and contemporary stories, the author shows that giving, even modestly, can have a lasting impact on lives and strengthen community bonds. Through sections dedicated to the spiritual and material benefits of generosity, he encourages readers to incorporate this value into their daily lives to enrich their relationship with God and with their neighbors.

Keywords: Generosity, faith, blessing, transformation, solidarity, act of giving, kindness, spirit of service, prosperity.

INTRODUCTION

It all started with a simple call one evening, an unexpected call from a friend living in Georgia, USA. She just wanted to check in on me, but during the conversation, she mentioned she had just celebrated her birthday. Surprised, I replied, "You celebrated your birthday without even telling me? Why? I would have loved to pray for you, even if I had nothing material to offer." She sincerely apologized, acknowledging that she had missed an important opportunity.

It was at that precise moment that I shared with her a reflection that is deeply dear to me: "A person's birthday is one of the best times to sow into their life." This simple exchange rekindled within me a powerful conviction: there are moments in everyone's life when our hearts are like fertile soil, ready to receive seeds. These special moments, such as birthdays, weddings, or moments of gratitude, are occasions where generosity can become much more than a gesture – it can become a seed that will bear abundant and unexpected fruit.

As I pondered this idea, my own birthday was approaching. I initially had no intention of celebrating it, but this conversation reminded me of an essential truth: a birthday is a privileged moment to allow those around us to sow into our life, just as we can sow into theirs. It was a turning point. I then decided to organize a celebration for my fifty-second birthday, not to receive, but to offer my friends and loved ones the opportunity to participate in a moment of sharing, exchange, and mutual blessing.

In reaching out to my closest friends, those with whom I had built relationships of trust, I proposed that each bring a contribution, a seed into my life through this celebration. This thanksgiving ceremony became much more than just a birthday: it transformed into a living testament to the power of mutual generosity. This book is the fruit of this unique experience, a lesson I have learned and wish to share: when you sow into the lives of others, there comes a time when those same people will come to sow into ours.

In the Christian faith, generosity is much more than a virtue; it is a direct reflection of God's love. Jesus himself taught that "it is more blessed to give than to receive" (Acts 20:35). By following the example of Christ, who gave his life for humanity, we understand that generosity goes far beyond material possessions. It includes time, prayer, and spiritual encouragement. Sowing into the lives of others is participating in a divine work of transformation.

This book invites you to reflect on the profound impact that generosity can have, both in your life and in the lives of others. Every generous gesture, every kind word, every act of support is a seed that will, sooner or later, bear fruit. As shown in the story of the widow of Zarephath or the apostle Paul, who was supported by generous believers, generosity not only blesses those who receive it but also those who practice it. It creates a virtuous cycle of blessings that transcends circumstances.

By sowing with love and faith, you participate in a deep transformation. This book is a guide, an invitation to fully embrace this principle: generosity changes lives, including yours.

PART I

CHAPTER ONE

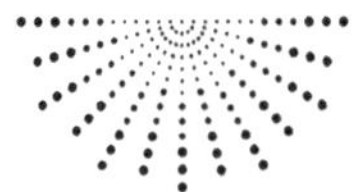

THE MEANING OF GENEROSITY

SECTION 1: DEFINITION OF GENEROSITY

Subsection 1.1: Etymology of the word "generosity"

The term generosity draws its roots from the Latin *generositas,* which originally referred to "nobility of birth" or an exalted quality of character. Over the centuries, this word has evolved to embody a virtue surpassing social distinctions: it is now associated with the act of giving abundantly, without any hope of reward. This semantic transformation highlights an inner nobility, a quality of the heart that, from a Christian perspective, translates into a profound commitment to others. Christian generosity, inspired by the example of Christ, goes beyond mere material giving; it reflects a spirit of kindness and compassion, a willingness to serve and support those around us, regardless of ties or expectations.

Thus, generosity, in its essence, embodies this moral nobility that elevates man, bringing him closer to the purity of divine love, a love that offers itself without limits and without conditions.

Subsection 1.2: Biblical Definition of Generosity

Generosity, according to the Bible, is not just an isolated act but a vocation deeply rooted in God's love and compassion. It is an active response to His goodness, a reflection of His heart towards humanity. Generosity is manifested through concrete and daily actions: feeding the hungry, clothing the needy, caring for the sick, and welcoming those who are alone or marginalized (Matthew 25:35-40). These actions, although simple, embody the divine call to love our neighbor as ourselves, because every act of generosity becomes a form of living worship, honoring God's presence in our world.

Moreover, the Bible teaches that generosity is a powerful force that transforms not only the lives of those who receive but also those who practice it. Proverbs 11:25 reminds: "A generous soul will be made rich, and he who waters will also be watered himself." Thus, by sowing generosity, we reap not only blessings for others, but we also grow in divine grace and abundance, strengthening our faith and connection with God. Generosity then becomes a path of personal transformation and communion with the divine, a gift that transcends human boundaries to touch souls and change lives.

SECTION 2: BIBLICAL EXAMPLES OF GENEROSITY

Subsection 2.1: The Story of the Widow of Zarephath (1 Kings 17:8-16)

The inspiring story of the widow of Zarephath illustrates the power of generosity, even in the face of scarcity. This woman, who had only a handful of flour and a few drops of oil, was confronted with a heartbreaking choice: to use her meager resources for herself and her son or to share them with a stranger, the prophet Elijah, in response to God's call. By choosing to give despite her lack, she not only demonstrated profound faith but also embodied the strength of unreserved generosity.

Her act of faith and selfless giving triggered an extraordinary miracle: an abundance divine, which ensured her survival and that of her son during the entire period of famine. Through this example, the Bible teaches us that even in our moments of vulnerability, an act of generosity can attract divine favor and open the door to unexpected blessings. The widow of Zarephath reminds us that true generosity is not measured by quantity but by the quality of the sacrifice and the faith that accompanies it.

Subsection 2.2: The Story of Zacchaeus (Luke 19:1-10)

The story of Zacchaeus illustrates the transformative power of divine grace and the deep impact that sincere generosity can have. Zacchaeus, as a tax collector, was perceived by society as a sinner and oppressor, rejected and scorned. But his encounter with Jesus turned his life upside down. In a gesture of love and acceptance, Jesus looked beyond his past actions and saw a man capable of transformation. Touched by this grace, Zacchaeus responded in a radical way: he not only decided to return everything he had taken unjustly, but also to give half of his possessions to the poor.

This act of generosity, motivated by the encounter with Jesus, shows how divine goodness can break the chains of selfishness and awaken in each of

us the desire to share with others. Zacchaeus's generosity thus becomes a concrete manifestation of his conversion, a living example of how God can inspire profound changes. By giving freely and unreservedly, Zacchaeus demonstrates that generosity, when motivated by love and grace, can truly change lives and impact those around us.

The lesson of Zacchaeus is clear: true generosity is an act of faith and transformation, a reflection of our commitment to God and our fellow man.

How Generosity Can Transform Lives: Dacet's Testimony

One of the most striking moments of my life, in terms of generosity, is the one I experienced with a young boy named Dacet. At only 12 years old, Dacet dreamed of becoming a doctor. But he faced financial obstacles that threatened to turn his dream into a mere illusion. Coming from a modest family, he could not afford the books necessary for his education, which seemed to compromise his chances of success.

One day, as I encountered him in my hometown, Limbé, he spoke to me about his academic performance, and I saw the spark of immense potential. He had good grades, but he confided that he could do much better if he had the necessary tools. Touched by his ambition and honesty, I made him a promise: "**If you continue to excel and maintain this motivation, I pledge to provide you with all the books you need each year.**" I offered him my support, not only for that year but for his entire educational journey.

With this help, Dacet brilliantly completed his secondary education. Yet, at the dawn of his university studies, Haiti was hit by a disaster, and the university had to close its doors. Despair took hold of him. It was as if his dream was once again collapsing. But I refused to let him sink. I gave him a book, The Magic of Thinking Big, which reignited his hope, and I gave him the opportunity to study abroad. He persevered and eventually became a doctor.

The day of his graduation, despite my professional obligations, I was able to attend this significant event. After the ceremony, during the celebration dinner, Dacet surprised me with a special gift: a plaque of honor. He looked me in the eye and said: "**Godfather, this plaque belongs to you.**" I was overwhelmed. It was not just a simple object but the symbol of all that generosity can accomplish.

This moment reminded me of a fundamental truth: **generosity transforms lives**. By offering simple help at a crucial moment, you not only change a person's life, but you plant a seed of lasting transformation. The happiness that Dacet felt in becoming a doctor is living proof that when we sow into the lives of others, we participate in an infinite chain of benefits.

And you? What seed will you plant today? You have the power to transform destinies, to sow hope, and to make dreams blossom where all seemed lost. Be the one who brings this light into others' lives. Generosity, as simple as it may be, creates an impact you cannot imagine.

CHAPTER TWO

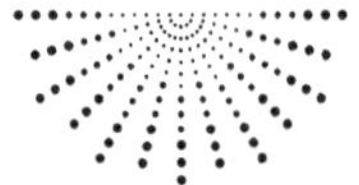

THE CALL TO GENEROSITY

SECTION 1: THE CALL TO SOW INTO THE LIVES OF OTHERS

Generosity goes far beyond mere material giving; it is a spiritual act that touches upon the very essence of our humanity, a deep expression of God's love manifested through our actions. In the Gospel of Luke, Jesus teaches us a fundamental principle: « Give, and it will be given to you. A good measure, pressed down, shaken together, and running over, will be poured into your lap » (Luke 6:38)

This principle of sowing and reaping is at the heart of Christian life. Each act of generosity becomes a seed planted in the garden of life, which, by divine grace, will bear abundant fruit.

By choosing to sow into the lives of others—whether through our time, resources, or love—we are not merely making an isolated gesture; we are actively contributing to the work of divine transformation. As the apostle Paul so aptly expressed, « Whoever sows generously will also reap generously » (2 Corinthians 9:6). Thus, generosity becomes an echo of God's grace, touching hearts and changing destinies, participating in the great mission of renewal and universal love.

Subsection 1.1: The Benefits of Generosity for the Giver

When we choose to be generous, we receive much more than what we give. The inner peace and joy that accompany an act of kindness cannot be quantified. As stated in Proverbs 11:25, "The one who waters will himself be watered". This means that each gift is a source of blessing, not only for the recipient but also for the giver. Studies even show that acts of generosity promote mental health, reduce stress, and strengthen social bonds.

Subsection 1.2: The Benefits of Generosity for the Receiver

Receiving an act of generosity often brings immediate comfort, but its benefits extend far beyond the present moment. Generosity has the power to revive hope, restore lost dignity, and provide new momentum toward the future. In the parable of the Good Samaritan (Luke 10:30-37), Jesus beautifully illustrates how a simple act of kindness can transform the life of a person left for dead. It is not only the physical relief that the Samaritan offers but also a silent message of human value and dignity.

Thus, every act of generosity is a seed planted in the heart of the receiver, often with deep and lasting repercussions.

Generosity does not merely satisfy an immediate need; it instills new hope and encourages the receiver to believe again in the goodness of life and in the capacity of others to provide help. By restoring courage and dignity, generosity becomes a powerful vector of personal transformation.

SECTION 2: THE OBSTACLES TO GENEROSITY

Subsection 2.1: The Fear of Lack

One of the main obstacles to generosity lies in the fear of lacking. We are often inclined to adopt a scarcity mindset, thinking that sharing what we have would jeopardize our own security. This feeling of vulnerability is human and understandable. However, it goes against divine promises. In the Gospel of Matthew (6:25-34), Jesus invites us to observe creation: the birds neither sow nor reap, yet they lack nothing. The flowers of the field neither labor nor spin, yet their beauty surpasses that of royal garments. Through this analogy, Jesus reminds us that if God provides for the needs of nature, He will certainly take care of each of us.

Adopting a perspective of trust in God rather than a vision of scarcity frees us to give without reserve. By transcending the fear of lack, we open the door to a life marked by faith and generosity, believing that what we give will be multiplied and that there will always be enough for everyone.

Subsection 2.2: Selfishness

Selfishness represents a major obstacle to the expression of generosity. Caught within the prism of our own needs and personal aspirations, it becomes easy to overlook the needs of others. Yet, Jesus' call to sacrificial love, as illustrated by His own giving on the cross (John 3:16), shows us a way where love transcends individual interests. Jesus did not just give; He offered Himself entirely, setting the highest example of sacrifice and selflessness.

Overcoming selfishness does not only mean giving up material goods, but also that human tendency that pushes us to prioritize our own interests. By abandoning this mentality, we enter a life of spiritual abundance, marked by authentic relationships and deep joy. Thus, each act of generosity becomes a step towards a more fulfilling life in harmony with the teachings of Jesus, where joy resides in self-giving and communion with others.

Real Story: The story of the woman who gave her last dollar to help a family

In a modest village, there lived a woman named Elza. With limited resources, she only had enough to buy a meager meal for herself and her family that day. But upon learning that her neighbors were going through even harder times and had nothing to eat, she made an extraordinary choice: she offered her last dollar to help them. This simple, humble, and yet powerful act allowed her neighbors to share a meal, warming not only their hearts but also those of the entire community.

This gesture, though seemingly small, resonated as an example of selfless kindness. Inspired by this act, the villagers also began to share with those in need. It was the beginning of a chain of generosity, where everyone felt called to give, even a little, to support their neighbor. Elza's generosity was ultimately rewarded beyond her expectations: shortly after, she was offered a stable job, which not only allowed her to provide for her family's needs but also to continue helping others, fueling the chain of solidarity she had initiated.

This story of Elza reminds us that generosity goes far beyond the act of giving. As Jesus teaches in Matthew 6:3-4, "Do not let your left hand know what your right hand is doing." True generosity comes from the heart, without expectation of return. By overcoming her own immediate needs to help others, Elza sowed a seed of goodness that blossomed in the hearts of the entire community. In return, life rewarded her altruism with unexpected abundance, highlighting that every act of kindness carries the potential to transform lives and sometimes even entire destinies.

Chapter conclusion:

This chapter highlights the biblical calls to generosity, emphasizing its benefits for both the giver and the receiver while addressing common obstacles to overcome. It concludes with an inspiring story, demonstrating that generosity, even in difficulty, can transform lives.

CHAPTER THREE

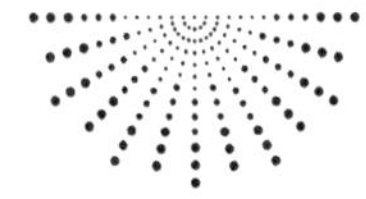

THE BENEFACTORS

SECTION 1: THE STORIES OF BENEFACTORS

In this chapter, we will discover the inspiring journeys of benefactors who marked their era with their acts of generosity. Each of them sowed in the lives of others in a way that profoundly impacted not only the beneficiaries but also an entire community.

Sub-section 1.1: The story of Nann

Nann was much more than just a generous man; he was a catalyst for transformation. Each year, he took a portion of his modest income to invest in the future of young people from disadvantaged backgrounds. For him, education was not a luxury but a powerful weapon capable of breaking the chains of poverty. Rather than simply offering money, Nann offered a chance, a door open to a better future. He firmly believed that by elevating these young people, he was changing not only their lives but also those of their community.

The years passed, and the fruits of his generosity began to manifest. Some of these young people, once hopeless, became doctors, teachers, entrepreneurs, and even local leaders. They not only succeeded in life but also understood the importance of giving back what they had received. Today, these former beneficiaries of Nann's help are spreading generosity in turn by supporting other young people in need, thus creating a ripple effect.

Nann's gesture touched hundreds, maybe even thousands of lives, proving that when you sow with love and intention, the harvests are abundant and continue to grow well beyond imagination.

Sub-section 1.2: The story of Pastor Nester

Pastor Nester was a man whose entire life reflected a profound conviction: that every act of generosity, no matter how small, could change the world. Inspired by James 1:27, he saw helping widows and orphans as a way to fully live his faith. Every month, without expecting recognition, he organized food distributions, bringing not only something to nourish the body but also something to warm the hearts.

Families in need knew that when Pastor Nester arrived, he did not come only with material provisions. He came with words of hope, kind advice, and, most importantly, attentive listening. For him, every life touched was a step towards a better world. He firmly believed that change starts with small acts, repeated with love.

One day, a woman, a widow with three children, remembered the pastor's visits. She declared, "It was not just the food, it was the strength he gave me. Thanks to him, I found the courage to face each day." That is how the pastor saw the world: a place where generosity could break the chains of despair and where every act, no matter how modest, had a lasting impact.

His story proves that simple acts, like a visit, a shared meal, or a comforting word, can truly make the world better.

Subsection 1.3: Thonn's Story - A Simple Gesture, an Unexpected Impact

It is sometimes easy to think that those who have succeeded in life, those who possess everything they need, do not need small gestures of attention. But the story I am going to share taught me that even the wealthiest can be deeply touched by generosity and that every gesture, no matter how simple, has an impact.

My friend Guy, a former player of Club Victory in Haiti, is a prosperous man. He owns a thriving business and lives comfortably. Every time I go to Haiti, he always welcomes me warmly. His wife makes sure I am well received, and he never hesitates to make me feel at home. Despite his success and apparent lack of needs, one day I decided to offer him a simple gesture of friendship.

Before my last trip to Haiti, I thought about bringing something for Guy. Nothing grand, just a pack of ties. When I arrived at his store, he was delighted to see me. I handed him the package, and he smiled upon seeing the ties. But after looking at this modest gift, he nodded, visibly moved.

Intrigued, I asked him why he reacted this way. What he told me deeply marked me: "You are the first person coming from abroad who brings me something."

This revelation surprised me. Guy was never lacking anything; he could have bought these ties himself. But this gesture, though simple, had a much deeper meaning for him. His wife had often pointed out that people coming from abroad never brought anything for him, thinking he did not need such attentions.

This experience taught me a valuable lesson: generosity is not just about giving to those in material need. Sometimes, even those who seem to have everything need to feel that they are important, that others care about them. This small gesture touched Guy in a way I could never have imagined.

Generosity is not measured by the material value of what one gives, but by the intention behind the gesture. It is not simply about helping those who lack everything, but also about showing those who have succeeded that we see them, that we appreciate them, and that we are there for them too.

Testimony of Generosity: Abraham and Tiline

My name is Tiline. It is often said that gratitude is a precious virtue, and today, I deeply feel the importance of this truth.

That morning will remain etched in my memory forever, as it marks the end of one journey and the beginning of a new chapter. Thanks to Abraham's generosity, my path took an unexpected and extraordinarily blessed turn.

A few months ago, I embarked on a project close to my heart: purchasing a piece of land to secure a better future for my family. But from the start, the obstacles seemed insurmountable. Funding this dream seemed impossible, and yet, it was not just about land but the foundation of my hopes and vision for tomorrow.

It was then that Abraham entered my life, with his heart wide open. Without hesitation, he offered me not only his financial support but also his unwavering encouragement. From the very first day, he believed in my project, even when I doubted myself. Abraham didn't just help me materially; he was by my side at every step, offering his time, wisdom, and advice, like a brother, a guide.

Today, thanks to him, I am finally the owner of this land, a land that symbolizes much more than material success: it embodies generosity, mutual aid, and trust between two souls. I remember every conversation with him, every moment when he told me: "Don't worry, everything will be fine. God is with you." These words, simple in appearance, carried immense weight in moments of doubt.

I haven't yet finalized the legal proceedings, but all that will be done soon. However, what's most important to me is this life lesson that Abraham offered me: true generosity doesn't lie solely in what one gives, but in the way one accompanies another on their journey, in moments of joy and in trials.

Today, I testify to Abraham's rare kindness. People like him are few and far between. His generosity has not only transformed my life, but it has also forever marked my family's destiny. I thank God for him, and I pray that everything he undertakes will be crowned with success. May his acts of kindness multiply and come back to him in the form of blessings.

Abraham, I can never thank you enough. May God fill you with prosperity and bless every step you take.

Testimony: "The Unexpected Return of Generosity"

Flora had always believed in the importance of sowing into the lives of others. As a young woman, she had opened her home to several girls in difficulty, offering them shelter, love, and sometimes financial support so they could pursue their studies. Among these girls, Clara, a reserved teenager, formed a special bond with Flora. Thanks to the help she received, Clara was able to complete her studies and soar towards a bright future.

Years later, when Flora's life was turbulent, she found herself at a crossroads. An aspiring novelist, she dreamed of leaving Abidjan for a foreign land where she could live in peace and pursue her art. However, resources and opportunities were scarce.

It was then that fate took an unexpected turn. One day, Flora received a call from Clara, whom she hadn't seen in years. Clara, now married to a French ambassador, had never forgotten Flora's kindness. Living in Paris, she offered to facilitate Flora's residency through her husband's influence.

"Flora, you helped me at a critical moment in my life, and I will never forget it. It's thanks to you that I became the woman I am today. Now, it's my turn to help you achieve your dream," Clara told her with sincere emotion.

Thanks to Clara and her husband, the French ambassador, Flora quickly obtained the necessary documents to live in France. There, she found peace, inspiration, and, finally, the opportunity to publish her novels. This act of generosity, sown years ago, returned to her, transformed into a blessing far greater than she could have imagined.

SECTION 2: THEIR MOTIVATION AND IMPACT

Sub-section 2.1: How They Were Touched by the Ceremony

At the Thanksgiving ceremony for my birthday, a deep sense of gratitude filled the air. My guests, who had come to celebrate the day, witnessed an event that exceeded the expectations of a simple birthday party. It was a sincere tribute to the bonds and gestures that, over the years, have shaped our community and strengthened our shared humanity.

Throughout the evening, testimonies revealed the impact my presence and actions had on their lives. Some friends shared how my advice or support helped them overcome important milestones. Others expressed their gratitude for moments of sharing and encouragement, which, even though they seemed trivial at the time, left a lasting imprint.

This gathering was not just a celebration: it was a powerful reminder of how every interaction, every smile, and every comforting word can sow a better future in the hearts of others. Upon leaving the ceremony, many expressed their desire to continue this chain of kindness, inspired by the celebration of the day and the unconditional love that emanated from it.

Subsection 2.2: How their generosity impacted my life and my environment

The generosity of my friends and benefactors not only enriched my life, it transformed an entire environment. What began as individual acts of support quickly took on the scale of a movement of kindness, where each action inspired the next. Each benefactor, by their example, awakened a desire to give in others, creating a chain of solidarity beyond what was initially imagined.

Their support gave me the strength to go further in my own commitments and inspired me to become a catalyst for change in my own right. By giving, they planted in me a renewed will to sow kindness around me, thus strengthening the bond between us and our community. In return, the beneficiaries, moved by this momentum, also began to give back, reflecting the biblical principle that "whoever sows generously will also reap generously" (2 Corinthians 9:6).

Thus, the impact of their generosity became a collective light that shines not only on me but radiates throughout our community, demonstrating that every act of kindness, no matter how modest, can transform lives and open horizons.

Chapter Conclusion:

The stories of the benefactors are living examples of the power of generosity. Each of them sowed into the lives of others with different resources, but all saw their seeds bear abundant fruit. Their stories remind us that generosity is a transformative force that can change lives, communities, and even generations.

CHAPTER FOUR

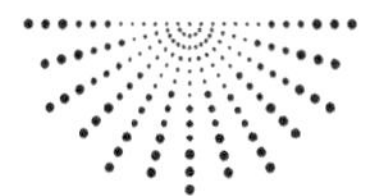

GRATITUDE AND RECOGNITION

SECTION 1: THE IMPORTANCE OF GRATITUDE

Gratitude is a virtue often overlooked in a world where we constantly chase the next achievement, the next goal. Yet it is essential to our spiritual and emotional well-being. The Apostle Paul reminds us in 1 Thessalonians 5:18 to "give thanks in all things," for gratitude brings us closer to God and helps us recognize His blessings in our lives. Cultivating gratitude changes our perspective and pushes us to see the hand of God even in difficult times.

Subsection 1.1: The benefits of gratitude for mental health

Numerous studies highlight that the regular practice of gratitude can profoundly improve our mental well-being. This mindset not only helps reduce our stress but also fosters greater serenity and strengthens our ability to cope with adversity. Psychology studies reveal that people actively cultivating gratitude tend to experience a greater joy of living and are less affected by depression.

On the spiritual level, gratitude enriches our relationship with God, inviting us to recognize His constant generosity. By reminding us that every blessing, big or small, comes from His will, gratitude nurtures a deep sense of inner peace and strengthens our faith. This spiritual aspect of gratitude transforms our perception of trials as opportunities for growth and acknowledgment of the divine.

Integrating gratitude into our daily life is not limited to improving our personal mindset; it also spreads positive waves around us, encouraging others to adopt a similarly appreciative attitude.

Subsection 1.2: The benefits of gratitude for relationships

Gratitude not only improves our state of mind; it is also a powerful lever to strengthen interpersonal relationships. By regularly expressing our appreciation to those around us, we solidify bonds and establish a climate of mutual trust. It becomes a virtuous circle of kindness that enriches our social and family network.

In the teachings of Jesus, the importance of gratitude is highlighted through the episode of the ten lepers healed, reported in the Gospel of Luke (17:11-19). Among the ten healed, only one returns to express his gratitude to Jesus. This parable highlights the crucial importance of not taking the benefits received for granted and openly acknowledging the actions of others. This act of gratitude is not only a sign of respect but also validates and reinforces the benefit received and the bond between the giver and the receiver.

By cultivating an attitude of gratitude, we open ourselves not only to a more fulfilling life but also to deeper and more sincere relationships. This active recognition encourages others to continue to act positively, thereby creating an environment where generosity and gratitude mutually nourish each other.

SECTION 2: EXAMPLES OF GRATITUDE IN THE BIBLE

The Bible is filled with stories that illustrate the importance of gratitude towards God and others. These narratives remind us that recognition is not only a natural response to God's goodness but also an act of faith that sets the stage for future blessings.

Subsection 2.1: The Story of the Woman Who Washed Jesus' Feet (Luke 7:36-50)

In the Gospel of Luke (7:36-50), we discover the poignant story of a sinful woman who, through an act of devotion, expresses her gratitude towards Jesus. Having received forgiveness for her sins, she approaches Him with a precious perfume, kneels down, sheds tears on His feet, and wipes them with her hair. By doing so, she transcends the social conventions of her time to express her deep and sincere appreciation.

This bold act of gratitude teaches us that understanding

God's grace elicits a tangible, unrestrained response in us and can even compel us to defy the gazes or judgments of others. The woman thus illustrates the transformative power of recognition, which goes far beyond words, revealing a faith and humility that touch the heart of God. This story reminds us that authentic gratitude, selflessly and shamelessly expressed, can not only strengthen our faith but also inspire those around us to recognize and honor the blessings they receive.

Ultimately, this story invites each of us to reflect: to what extent are we willing to express our gratitude to God and others, even if it challenges us to go beyond social conventions?

Subsection 2.2: The Story of David Thanking God for His Deliverance (Psalm 18)

David embodies an inspiring example of gratitude in the Bible. In Psalm 18, he fervently expresses his thanks to God after being delivered from his enemies. This psalm is a song of recognition that celebrates God's faithfulness, strength, and protection in the darkest moments. David does not hide his gratitude: he proclaims it publicly, thus testifying to the importance of giving glory to God for His interventions in our lives.

Through this psalm, David shows us that gratitude goes beyond inner feelings; it manifests through visible words and actions. Expressing our thanks publicly, as David did, inspires others to also recognize the benefits they have received. This act of faith reminds us that witnessing God's faithfulness strengthens our own faith and that of those who surround us, creating a chain of gratitude that touches the entire community.

This story of active gratitude invites every believer to ask: how can I, in turn, celebrate the benefits of God in my life in a visible and uplifting way for those around me?

Chapter Conclusion

Gratitude transforms our perspective on life. By thanking God for His blessings, large and small, we learn to live with a lighter heart and to appreciate more the gifts we receive. Moreover, by expressing our thanks to others, we sow seeds of kindness and understanding, thereby strengthening our relationships and our bond with God.

CHAPTER FIVE

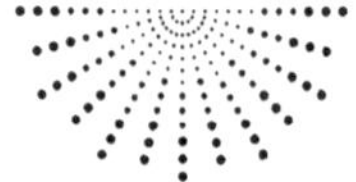

THE BENEFITS OF GENEROSITY

SECTION 1: SPIRITUAL BENEFITS

Generosity is not just an external act; it has profound effects on our spiritual life. When we give to others, we open the door to greater intimacy with God and spiritual growth. Jesus himself teaches us in Acts 20:35: "It is more blessed to give than to receive." This happiness comes from our alignment with the heart of God, who is generous by nature. Through generosity, we experience inner transformation.

Subsection 1.1: Spiritual Growth

Generosity is a powerful lever for spiritual growth, as it helps us detach from material possessions and strengthen our relationship with God. By giving, we demonstrate our trust in divine providence, believing that God watches over our needs. This act of faith teaches us to rely more on Him than on our possessions.

The Bible is filled with promises for those who give with an open heart. 2 Corinthians 9:6 states: "The person who sows sparingly will also reap sparingly, and the person who sows generously will also reap generously." This spiritual truth reminds us that generosity creates a space where God can act and multiply His blessings in our life. Giving is not limited to a material act; it is a path to deepen our faith, where each act of generosity enriches our soul and opens our hearts to divine benevolence. Thus, by planting seeds in the lives of others, we also cultivate our own spiritual growth, transforming our lives and those around us.

Subsection 1.2: Inner Peace

Generosity is a powerful source of inner peace. By giving, we break the chains of fear of lack to embrace a mentality of abundance, which lightens the heart and soothes the mind. This spiritual tranquility finds its source in the trust we place in God, firmly believing that He will provide for all our needs in return.

Proverbs 11:25 perfectly illustrates this truth: "The generous soul will be enriched, and he who waters will also be watered himself." In other words, generosity enriches both the giver and the receiver, not by creating a void, but by filling our life with the satisfaction of doing God's will. By being generous, we cultivate a lasting peace that transcends material concerns, aligning us with divine benevolence and strengthening our faith.

SECTION 2: MATERIAL BENEFITS

In addition to spiritual blessings, generosity can also bring material benefits. The Bible promises that God will take care of those who are generous. Although it is not a matter of giving to receive, the Scriptures show us that material blessing is often the fruit of a generous heart.

Subsection 2.1: Abundance

Generosity acts as a lever to trigger a cycle of abundance in our lives. By giving with a sincere heart, we express a deep faith in divine provision, demonstrating that we believe God will meet our needs beyond what we can imagine. This principle of abundance, illustrated in Malachi 3:10, where God says: "Try me in this, says the Lord of hosts, and see if I will not open for you the floodgates of heaven", reveals that generosity is not an isolated act, but a seed planted in the spiritual realm.

Each sincere act of giving thus becomes a seed that bears fruit, triggering a divine return in the form of blessings. This cycle of harvest and abundance reminds us that God does not simply provide but gives in abundance. By giving generously, we experience this divine promise firsthand, learning to live in fullness, free from the fear of lack, and in communion with a renewed faith in God's faithfulness.

Subsection 2.2: Prosperity

Generosity towards others, particularly the needy, is a spiritual key that unlocks the doors to divine prosperity.

Proverbs 19:17 states: "He who has pity on the poor lends to the Lord, and He will pay back what he has given." In other words, each act of kindness is like an investment in a "heavenly bank" that guarantees fruitful returns. This prosperity is not limited to financial gains: it can result in unexpected opportunities, security in times of crisis, or blessings that meet our material and spiritual needs.

Thus, divine prosperity is much more than simple material enrichment. It represents a surge of gratitude and blessing that enriches the giver's life, transforming each act of love into a seed of prosperity, not only for the receiver but also for the giver.

Testimony: How Generosity Brought Me Prosperity

Jericho, a young man of 26, had experienced a difficult childhood. From a very young age, he had to leave elementary school because his father refused to pay for his tuition. This lack of family support could have led him to bitterness, but Jericho was not the type to be discouraged. Despite his own trials, he developed a rare quality: generosity. He always shared what he could with others, even if he himself had very little.

Jericho met many young people in his neighborhood who, like him, were facing financial difficulties. He shared his meager savings with those who needed to buy school supplies or just a meal. His generosity was genuine, expecting nothing in return. He saw it as an act of faith, believing that God blesses those who give with an open heart.

One day, a businessman, touched by Jericho's reputation, heard about his story. Impressed by his kindness despite his own challenges, this man offered him a job opportunity in his company. It was not just a job; it was the beginning of a transformation. Thanks to this open door, Jericho was able to return to studies, obtain professional training, and eventually embark on a prosperous career.

Jericho's generosity towards others, even in his darkest moments, eventually opened pathways of blessing he had never imagined. This simple act of sharing echoed, triggering a chain of goodness and blessings in his own life. His story shows that there is power in giving and that God, in His faithfulness, always provides at the right time.

This testimony illustrates that generosity is not just an isolated act but a catalyst for spiritual and material prosperity. Jericho is living proof that when you give without counting, blessings come in an unexpected and overflowing way.

Chapter conclusion:

This chapter illustrates that generosity, while primarily a spiritual act, also generates material benefits. By sowing into the lives of others, we not only meet an immediate need, but we also participate in a divine process of blessing and abundance.

CHAPTER SIX

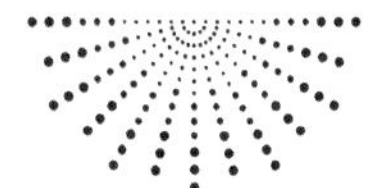

THE CHALLENGES OF GENEROSITY

SECTION 1: THE OBSTACLES TO GENEROSITY

Generosity, though it is a noble virtue, is not always easy to practice. Many obstacles stand in our way when we decide to give, be it fears, limiting beliefs, or social pressures. These challenges that we have already seen above, can sometimes discourage us, but by recognizing and overcoming these obstacles, we open ourselves to a more fulfilled life aligned with divine principles. It is really important to emphasize these obstacles because they can handicap us in our desire to be generous.

Sub-section 1.1: The fear of lack

One of the main obstacles to generosity is the fear of lack. We often live in a scarcity mentality, where the idea of giving seems to threaten our own financial security. However, this fear is contrary to biblical teachings that remind us that God is our provider. In Matthew 6:31-33, Jesus exhorts us not to worry about what we will eat or drink but to seek first the kingdom of God. By overcoming this fear, we trust in the promise that God will provide for all our needs. Our generous Father can help us drive them away.

Sub-section 1.2: Selfishness

Another major obstacle to generosity is selfishness, this tendency to focus solely on one's own needs and desires. In a society focused on consumption and individual success, selfishness can quickly become a barrier to altruism. But Jesus calls us to love our neighbor as ourselves (Mark 12:31), a command that invites us to go beyond selfishness to meet the needs of others.

SECTION 2: HOW TO OVERCOME THESE CHALLENGES

Despite the obstacles, generosity is a spiritual discipline that we can cultivate with God's help. By praying and practicing trust in His provision, we can overcome our fears and develop a generous heart.

Sub-section 2.1: Prayer

Prayer is an essential pillar for cultivating a spirit of generosity. In praying, we enter a deep communion with God, a space where our fears and uncertainties can be laid down with confidence. Prayer allows us to express our concerns about giving and to receive the peace and strength needed to give freely. As Philippians 4:6 says: "Do not be anxious about anything; but in everything, by prayer and petition, with thanksgiving, present your requests to God."

This passage teaches us that prayer aligns our will with God's, reminding us that our generosity flows from His goodness and provision. Thus, prayer becomes a catalyst, transforming our hesitations into active faith and a generosity freed from fears so that we can sow into the lives of others with joy and assurance.

Sub-section 2.2: Trust in God

To live an authentic generosity, it is essential to nurture an unshakeable trust in God. Faith in His provision allows us to give with a heart free from worries. Proverbs 3:5-6 exhorts us as follows: "Trust in the Lord with all your heart and lean not on your own understanding." This verse reminds us to let go of our own fears and place every need in the hands of God.

By entrusting God with the care of providing for our needs, we transform our perception of giving: it is no longer a sacrifice, but a demonstration of faith. This trust frees us from the fear of lack and encourages us to sow into the lives of others with a generous spirit, certain that our Heavenly Father constantly watches over us and will not fail to bless us in return.

Chapter Conclusion:

Generosity can be a challenge, but by overcoming obstacles such as the fear of lacking and selfishness, we become instruments of God's grace in this world. Through prayer and trust in God, we can cultivate a spirit of generosity that not only blesses others but also transforms us.

CHAPTER SEVEN

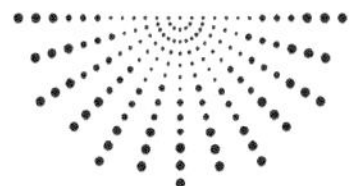

GENEROSITY IN EVERYDAY LIFE

SECTION 1: HOW TO INTEGRATE GENEROSITY INTO DAILY LIFE

Generosity should not be reserved for big occasions or exceptional moments. It should be part of our daily life, in small things as well as in big ones. Every day, we have the opportunity to sow into the lives of others through simple but meaningful gestures. The Bible teaches us to "show kindness and mutual love" (Hebrews 13:16). It is therefore important to turn generosity into a daily habit that reflects God's love through our actions.

Sub-section 1.1: Small Gestures

It is not necessary to possess wealth or sacrifice considerable time to express generosity. Sometimes, the simplest gestures—a smile, attentive listening, or a word of comfort—

carry a profound impact. Jesus, through His teachings and acts, reminds us that every act of kindness, even the most modest, can produce abundant fruits in the heart of the one who receives it.

In Matthew 25:40, He underscores this truth by saying: "Truly I tell you, whatever you did for one of the least of these brothers and sisters of mine, you did for me." This verse invites us to recognize that small gestures, though discreet, have transformative power and testify to our love for God and for others. A seed of kindness, sown with sincerity, can indeed make kindness and comfort flourish around us, influencing lives in a subtle yet lasting way.

Sub-section 1.2: Regular Giving

Incorporating regular giving, be it financial, time, or skills, to charities, churches, or directly to people in need is a powerful way to make generosity an integral part of our daily lives.

These consistent gestures demonstrate that generosity is not just an isolated act but becomes a true commitment. Regular giving urges us to think more deeply about the needs of others and invites us to show sustained kindness.

By cultivating this habit, one also develops a spirit of abundance, convinced that every gift, however modest, contributes to the community's well-being and strengthens human connections. Giving regularly transforms generosity into a lifestyle and a reflection of our commitment to the common good.

SECTION 2: EXAMPLES OF GENEROSITY IN EVERYDAY SITUATIONS

Generosity can take simple and everyday forms, yet its impact can be profound and lasting. Here are two examples that show how acts of kindness can transform not only moments but also lives.

Sub-section 2.1: The story of Rose, a young woman who gave up her seat

In a crowded bus during rush hour, Rose, an observant young woman, notices an elderly lady

standing, visibly exhausted from her day. Without hesitation, she gets up to offer her seat. This seemingly simple gesture transformed the day of the old lady who, for some time, had felt almost invisible amidst the hustle of urban life. The gratitude in her eyes went far beyond a mere thank you; it was a reminder of her dignity and existence.

This simple act triggered a chain reaction. Inspired by Rose's generosity, other passengers began to be more considerate: some offered to carry bags, others showed patience and let those in a hurry pass. This act of kindness infused a wave of courtesy in this bus, reminding everyone that a single act of kindness can transform the atmosphere and encourage a wave of collective generosity.

Sub-section 2.2: The story of the person who helped a neighbor

Leo often watched Joel, his elderly neighbor, struggling to

mow his lawn under the scorching sun. One day, unable to bear seeing him struggle any longer, Leo mustered up his courage and offered to help him. What began as a simple gesture of assistance quickly became a weekly ritual. But the benefits of this act of generosity went far beyond the well-kept appearance of the lawn.

Over time, a deep friendship developed between them. Joel, who had once suffered from loneliness, now eagerly anticipated these shared moments. Together, they exchanged stories, laughter, and life advice, creating a strong and authentic human bond. This simple act of generosity by Leo was not just physical help; it was also a source of emotional comfort and mutual support.

By helping Joel, Leo demonstrated that generosity has the power to transform lives, not only through visible acts but also through the deep connections it creates. Genuine help touches the heart and nurtures the soul, reminding us that humanity flourishes in these acts of sincere attention.

These examples remind us that generosity doesn't need to be spectacular to be powerful. Each small gesture counts and has the potential to bring about lasting change in the lives of others.

Chapter Conclusion:

Generosity in everyday life manifests through simple and regular acts. It does not require great means but a heart willing to serve. Each day is an opportunity to sow into the lives of others and to participate in the divine work by turning small gestures into great blessings.

CHAPTER EIGHT

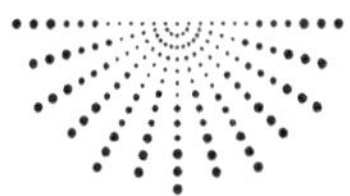

SERVANTS OF GOD AND GENEROSITY

SECTION 1: THE IMPORTANCE OF SOWING INTO THE LIVES OF GOD'S SERVANTS

The Bible teaches us the importance of supporting those who are in God's service. God's servants, whether pastors, missionaries, or church volunteers, dedicate their lives to the Lord's work. They need the spiritual and material support of the community to fulfill their mission. In Galatians 6:6, it is written: "Let the one who is taught the word share all good things with the one who teaches." By helping God's servants, we contribute to the spreading of the Gospel and bless those who are devoted to the kingdom.

Sub-section 1.1: The Benefits of Generosity for God's Servants

God's servants face daily challenges, whether spiritual or

material, and the support of their community is a precious source of encouragement and relief. By providing them with our help, whether through material donations, prayers, or simple moral support, we allow them to fully dedicate themselves to their mission without the anxiety of financial or material concerns.

When we decide to support a servant of God, we engage in an act of generosity with profound repercussions. Not only does it lighten his personal burdens, but our contribution also bears spiritual fruit in every soul touched by his ministry. This gesture is much more than a one-time aid; it becomes a lasting spiritual investment that continues to influence the lives of those who benefit from his work. Generosity towards the servants of God creates a virtuous circle where community support strengthens their impact, reminding us that every gift, however humble, contributes to a greater and transcendent mission.

Subsection 1.2: Biblical examples of generosity towards the servants of God

The Bible is full of examples of generosity towards the servants of God, where simple gestures of support turn into abundant blessings. In the Old Testament, the widow of Zarephath shows generosity by offering her last provisions to the prophet Elijah. Despite her poverty, she puts her faith in God by sharing what she has, and in return, God blesses her by multiplying her flour and oil, thus ensuring her a miraculous sustenance (1 Kings 17:8-16). This story teaches us that even the smallest act of generosity, when done with faith, can bring about unexpected blessings.

In the New Testament, we discover figures like Lydia, a merchant of purple, who, touched by Paul's teaching, opens her home to welcome him and his companions. This support, although simple, allows Paul and Silas to continue their mission with a mind free from material worries (Acts 16:14-15). Through these examples, the Bible shows that every act of generosity towards a servant of God is not only material support but also a spiritual investment that bears fruit for the giver and the entire community.

SECTION 2: EXAMPLES OF GENEROSITY TOWARDS THE SERVANTS OF GOD

Subsection 2.1: The story of the widow who gave to Elijah (1 Kings 17:8-16)

The story of the widow of Zarephath is one of the most powerful demonstrations of faith and generosity towards a servant of God. Despite her extremely limited resources and bleak prospects of famine, this woman made an act of faith by sharing her last provisions with the prophet Elijah. By obeying the divine instruction, she showed that she trusted God beyond her own immediate needs. This act of generosity, in conditions where everything seemed lost, triggered a miraculous blessing: God multiplied her flour and oil, ensuring she and her son were fed throughout the drought period.

This story teaches us that God honors acts of generosity, even the most modest ones, towards His servants. The widow's faithfulness not only provided for their material needs but also strengthened their faith and their connection with God. This example inspires those who, despite their own challenges, choose to sow into others' lives with faith, knowing that God never remains indifferent to such sacrifices.

Subsection 2.2: The story of the woman who helped Paul and Silas (Acts 16:14-15)

Lydia, a merchant of purple from Thyatira, embodies generosity towards the servants of God. When Paul and Silas arrived in her city, she was touched by their message and opened her heart to the Lord. Her faith moved her to act: she invited them into her home, offering valuable support for their mission. This warm welcome was not just a gesture of hospitality; it was an act of faith that contributed to the expansion of the Gospel in her region.

Lydia's example shows that generosity towards the servants of God is an act of cooperation with the divine plan. By supporting those who share the word of God, we sow into the Kingdom, indirectly influencing lives and strengthening our own relationship with God. Whether through material resources or a welcoming attitude, our support becomes a channel through which divine blessing spreads around us and beyond.

Testimony: How generosity supported the ministry of a young pastor in Passe-Catabois, Northwest Haiti

After completing my seminary studies, I was driven by a deep conviction: to serve God by establishing a mission field in a remote area. This is how I settled in the communal section of Passe-Catabois, in the Northwest of Haiti, a region where the Gospel had little resonance. The challenges were numerous: geographical isolation, lack of resources, and above all, the skepticism of some locals towards this new mission.

However, it was thanks to the generosity of the local community and the church that supported me that this ministry could not only survive but thrive. I remember a particular moment when we could no longer afford to continue the church construction. I was discouraged, thinking that everything we had undertaken might collapse. That's when a family from the community, living in extreme modesty, decided to give the few resources they had saved to contribute to the progress of the work. This act of faith and sacrifice was the starting point for a wave of generosity. Gradually, other villagers, inspired by this act, provided their help: some offered wood, others time to work on the site, and thus, the construction could be completed.

But it was not just a matter of material construction. Generosity also helped build strong relationships within the community. At every stage, God's hand was manifested through the gifts of those who had little but gave with a generous heart. Thanks to this solidarity, the ministry at Passe-Catabois could touch many lives. Today, the church is a place of gathering and living faith, and I am convinced that without the generosity of this small community, this ministry would never have reached this scale.

This testimony shows that generosity, even in situations of poverty, can transform lives and make ministries flourish where they are least expected.

. . .

Chapter conclusion:

This chapter highlights the importance of supporting God's servants and the blessings that result. By sowing into their lives, we directly contribute to God's work on earth and in return, receive divine promises.

CHAPTER NINE

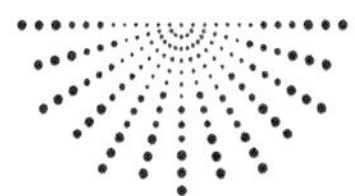

GOD'S BLESSINGS ON GIVERS

SECTION 1: THE BIBLICAL PROMISE OF BLESSING FOR GIVERS

God is generous and invites His children to be likewise. The Bible is filled with promises of blessing for those who practice generosity. Giving with a pure heart not only helps others but also attracts divine favor. Proverbs 11:25 says: "The generous soul will be made rich, and he who waters will also be watered himself." This promise emphasizes the idea that every act of generosity brings a divine return, a multiplication of blessings in the giver's life.

Sub-section 1.1: Biblical Verses on God's Blessing

The Bible highlights the importance of giving with a sincere and joyful heart. In 2 Corinthians 9:7, it says: "Let each one give as he purposes in his heart, not grudgingly or of necessity; for God loves a cheerful giver." This verse shows that for God, the attitude with which we give is more important than the amount. God values a gift driven by love and sincerity, and He responds to this generosity by multiplying His blessings in our lives.

By giving with a pure heart, we not only perform an act of kindness; we place ourselves in a divine flow of grace and abundance. God, in return, opens doors and showers blessings on those who, with love and without constraints, commit to sowing into the lives of others. This spiritual principle ensures that the blessing is not only material but also impacts our peace, joy, and spiritual fulfilment.

Sub-section 1.2: Biblical Examples of Blessing for Givers

The Bible is full of accounts where generosity leads to abundant blessings. Abraham, known for his faith and generosity, did not hesitate to offer the best part of what he possessed. For this obedience and largesse, he was called "friend of God" and received the promise of a lineage as numerous as the stars, becoming the father of a great nation (Genesis 12:2).

Solomon also illustrates the impact of generosity. After offering sacrifices in abundance, God granted him not only the wisdom he had requested but also unmatched wealth and honors (1 Kings 3:10-13). Similarly, Job, despite his trials, demonstrated great faith and trust in God, which led to an even greater restoration of his possessions and family.

These stories show that generosity, when aligned with the divine will, attracts God's blessings, transforming not only the lives of the givers but also those around them.

SECTION 2: TESTIMONIALS OF BLESSING

Generosity is not only an act of faith but also a powerful path to blessings. Many believers have seen God's hand at work after giving with a sincere and open heart. Their testimonials reflect not only God's faithfulness but also the immense impact a generous life can have on their destiny.

Subsection 2.1: Jacques' Testimony

Jacques, a family man working in a small business, had long felt the need to give to a charity, despite the financial difficulties he was going through. One day, while listening to a sermon on generosity, he decided to make a significant donation to an organization that helped underprivileged children. This gesture of faith, though uncertain materially, brought him great inner peace.

A few weeks later, when he least expected it, Jacques received a job offer from a prestigious company, an opportunity far beyond what he had hoped for. Not only did this offer significantly improve his finances, but it also provided him with a balance between his professional and family life. This powerful testimony shows that divine blessing can manifest in unexpected ways, often when we take a step of faith to sow into the lives of others.

Subsection 2.2: Carmelle's Testimony

Carmelle, a committed member of her local church ministry, had always believed that sowing into God's kingdom was a way to receive back much more than was given. Although she was going through times of great financial uncertainty, she continued to regularly contribute to the church, convinced that God would provide for her needs.

Over time, Carmelle saw her finances miraculously stabilized. Every time she gave, she received unexpected blessings: job opportunities, discounts on her bills, and even unforeseen support from relatives and community members. This cycle of blessing confirmed in her heart that every gift, however small, can lead to much greater abundance, provided it is given with a sincere heart. Her testimony is a vibrant example of how God takes care of those who trust Him and how generosity opens the doors to miracles

Chapter conclusion:

These stories show that generosity, far from being a sacrifice, is a key to unlocking unexpected blessings in our lives. Jacques and Carmelle are living proof that giving with faith and humility attracts divine favor in a powerful and transformative way.

The Bible teaches us that divine blessing follows generosity. By giving, we open the door to provision, inner peace, and prosperity. These testimonials and biblical examples encourage us to live a life of giving, confident that God will provide for all our needs in return.

CHAPTER TEN

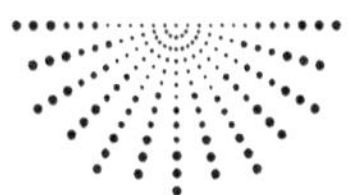

CONCLUSION AND CALL TO ACTION

SECTION 1: SUMMARY OF KEY POINTS

Throughout the pages of this book, we have explored the power of generosity and how it can transform not only the lives of those who receive but also those of the givers. Generosity is a divine principle rooted in the Bible, and it manifests itself in various aspects of daily life. Whether through material donations or a simple act of kindness, every act of generosity creates a lasting impact.

Subsection 1.1: Generosity as a Christian Value

As we have seen throughout this book, generosity is at the heart of Jesus Christ's teachings. It is more than just a virtue; it is an expression of God's love for humanity. By giving freely, we reflect the image of God, who gave His only Son for the salvation of all. Generosity is a direct response to God's love and a tangible way to manifest our faith.

Subsection 1.2: The Benefits of Generosity for the Giver and the Receiver

The benefits of generosity are numerous and affect both the giver and the receiver. The receiver is often relieved, encouraged, and even transformed by an act of kindness. As for the giver, they discover greater inner peace, a deeper spiritual connection with God, and often, unexpected material blessings. Generosity is a cycle of blessing that benefits all who participate in it.

SECTION 2: CALL TO ACTION

Now that you have explored the many facets of generosity, it is time to put into practice what you have learned. This book is not just a theoretical guide; it is a call to action, an invitation to make generosity a way of life.

Subsection 2.1: How to Incorporate Generosity into Your Life

The first step to becoming a generous person is to make conscious decisions in everyday life. Start with small gestures —helping a neighbor, giving a little time to a cause, or even lending a listening ear to someone in need. These small acts, when practiced regularly, can change your heart and open the door to greater opportunities for generosity.

Subsection 2.2: How to Encourage Others to Be Generous

Your example of a generous life can be a powerful testimony to encourage others to follow the same path. Talk about the joy and blessings you have received through your acts of generosity and inspire those around you to engage in this path. Generosity is contagious, and by planting this seed in the lives of others, you will help create a more loving and compassionate community.

Chapter conclusion: Generosity is a powerful force that can transform lives, communities, and generations. It is both an act of faith and a practical tool for bringing God's love into this world. May this book inspire you to sow abundantly into the lives of others, knowing that each seed will produce a bountiful harvest.

CONCLUSION OF THE FIRST PART

Generosity is more than just an action; it is a way of living, a philosophy that reflects the heart of God. Through this book, we have explored the many facets of generosity, its spiritual and material benefits, and its transformative power in the lives of others and in ours. To give is not only to offer material resources; it is to share love, compassion and sow seeds of kindness that will bloom in the future.

Each of us is called to be generous, not out of obligation, but as a natural response to the love that God shows us daily. The Bible encourages us to give wholeheartedly, with joy, knowing that every gesture, big or small, is precious in God's eyes. The blessing that accompanies generosity is often beyond what we can imagine, for God promises to take care of those who take care of others.

Thus, may this book be a source of inspiration to encourage you to sow in the lives of others with faith and love, knowing that each seed you plant will be multiplied. Generosity transforms not only the recipients but also the givers, offering them a life richer in divine blessings and inner peace.

PART II

INSPIRING FIGURES:

A GALLERY OF GENEROUS HEARTS

In this second part of *Sowing Seeds of Generosity: Changing Lives, Shaping Destinies,* we invite you to discover a gallery of generous souls whose lives and actions illustrate the power of altruism. These inspiring portraits are not just testimonies of kindness but living examples of how an open heart can transform the world around it. Each person featured here has sown with love and conviction into the lives of others, often without expecting anything in return, and their acts have left an indelible mark.

As you browse through these pages, you will discover that generosity is not only measured in terms of material gifts but also by the ability to touch hearts, uplift spirits, and bring hope and light in times of need. May this gallery be a source of inspiration for each of us, reminding us that every gesture, however small, can be a seed that changes lives and destinies.

GALLERY OF GENEROUS PEOPLE

JOSE SAINT-HILAIRE

A GENEROUS HEART IN THE SERVICE OF OTHERS

Doctor Jose Saint-Hilaire is a man whose generosity transcends boundaries and circumstances. From our youth at the Evangelical Baptist School of Limbé, then to the Notre-Dame College of Cap-Haïtien, he has always shown sincere dedication to those around him. Our bond has lasted beyond the years and miles. Upon my arrival in the United States, he welcomed me warmly, taking care of my food and financial needs, never expecting anything in return. His kindness and support have been extended not only to me but also to members of his church and everyone who crosses his path. He is a man of unmatched generosity, inspiring each of us to demonstrate the same kindness.

Jose Saint-Hilaire perfectly embodies the spirit of a devoted servant, capable of sowing seeds of love and assistance in the lives of others. His most precious gift is giving with a pure heart, expecting nothing in return. What distinguishes him is not only what he offers materially but also the encouragement he provides, the dignity he restores, and the inspiration he sparks around him.

The name Jose Saint-Hilaire resonates like a hymn of kindness and love. Each letter of his first name unveils a precious aspect of his personality and impact in our lives.

Let us discover together what each letter of his name reveals, as a tribute to his great generosity.

Acrostic - Jose Saint-Hilaire:

Joyful in service, always giving his best.
Open-hearted, spreading kindness wherever he goes.
Strength rooted in faith, inspiring many.
Elevating others with his unwavering support.

Sowing seeds of hope in every action.
Active in generosity, a beacon of love.
Integrity defines his every step.
Nurturing lives with wisdom and care.
Transforming destinies through acts of compassion.

Hopeful and humble, a true servant of God.
Illuminating paths for others to follow.
Leaving a legacy of love and faith.

Always a helping hand to those in need.
Inspirational in both word and deed.
Reflecting God's grace in his journey.
Eternal gratitude for his generosity.

Doctor Jose Saint-Hilaire's journey is a source of inspiration for all. His ability to give without limits, to lend a hand with love and kindness, is an invitation to live a life marked by generosity. Through his actions, he shows us that true power lies not in what one possesses, but in what one offers. He is a light, a blessing for those fortunate enough to cross his path. May his example continue to illuminate our lives and encourage everyone to sow in the lives of others with the same kindness.

PASTOR ERNEST JEAN

A GENEROSITY THAT SHINES BEYOND BOUNDARIES

Pastor Ernest Jean is much more than a spiritual guide: he embodies a model of generosity and humanity. His ability to give without expecting anything in return has touched the lives of many people, whether in Haiti or in Miami. By founding and leading several churches, he has offered thousands of souls a place of peace, hope, and encouragement.

Convinced that education is a seed for the future, Pastor Ernest also founded a school, giving young people the opportunity to chart their own path. His constant dedication to helping others, without ever expecting anything in return, makes him a true beacon of light, leaving an indelible mark on the hearts of those he meets.

His commitment to his community, his faith, and the values he embodies inspire everyone who crosses his path. Pastor Ernest is the living embodiment of generosity in action, a man whose selfless actions continue to inspire a generation to sow seeds in the lives of others as well.

To capture the full extent of his impact, each letter of his name reveals a unique facet of his character, like a mosaic of qualities that, together, paint the picture of a man of faith and kindness. Let us discover together what each letter of the name **Ernest** signifies in this life of service and light.

Acrostic of Ernest Jean:
Preaching hope with passion and humility.
Acting with faith, serving tirelessly.
Strengthened by God's word, leading with love.
Transforming lives through acts of kindness.
Elevating souls by showing Christ's example.
Uniting communities with unwavering commitment.
Representing God's love in every gesture.

Empowered by grace, inspiring countless lives.
Renewing hope wherever he goes.
Nurturing faith in every heart.
Encouraging others to walk in generosity.
Sowing peace and joy as a true shepherd.
Trusting God in every mission.

Joyfully serving with purpose and devotion.
Exemplifying leadership rooted in faith.
Always a source of light in the darkest times.
Never ceasing to reflect God's love.

Thus, through each of these qualities, Pastor Ernest Jean embodies generosity in action. His commitment inspires a generation to follow his example, planting seeds of kindness and faith in the hearts of others. May his journey continue to illuminate the path of all who aspire to give and make a lasting difference.

PASTOR JEAN-ROBERT BILDA

A GENEROUS AND VISIONARY LEADER AT THE SERVICE OF THE COMMUNITY

Jean-Robert Bilda embodies generosity, kindness, and exceptional leadership. As the president of the Union of Baptist Churches of Haiti (UEBH), he works tirelessly for the growth of his community, especially for the youth of Saintard. A great entrepreneur and devoted pastor, Jean-Robert founded a school to provide the youth with the necessary tools to face life with confidence and dignity. Always ready to support the most vulnerable, he gives his time, energy, and abilities without counting to help them reach their full potential.

His natural leadership and sharp sense of responsibility are evident in every act of service. His generous approach deeply inspires those around him, fostering an atmosphere of respect and mutual aid. Jean-Robert Bilda is a model of selflessness, whose altruism encourages everyone to act for the good of others. Discover the exceptional qualities of this admirable man through each letter of his name.

Acrostic of Jean-Robert Bilda:

Patient in his faith, leading by example.
Anchor of hope for his community.
Strong in spirit, gentle in action.
Trusted shepherd, guiding with love.
Every word filled with divine wisdom.
Uplifting others with his generosity.
Radiating God's grace in all his deeds.

Just and compassionate in every encounter.
Embodying faith through consistent service.
Always seeking the well-being of others.
Never wavering in his mission to serve.

Reflecting the values of Christ in his life.
Open-hearted in every act of giving.
Believing in the power of transformation.
Empowering others to find their purpose.
Remembered for his enduring kindness.
Tireless in his commitment to God's call.

May the example of Jean-Robert Baldi continue to inspire each of us to serve with generosity and humility so that the impact of our actions resonates far beyond our lives.

FLORENCE PETIT-FRÈRE

AN UNFAILING SOURCE OF GENEROSITY

Florence Petit-Frère embodies the true essence of dedication and generosity. During her time at the Tabernacle Baptist Church, she passionately invested in mentoring young girls, offering them more than just advice: she imparted a part of herself, an invaluable source of inspiration. Every moment she spent supporting them was a seed planted in their future, a seed of love and kindness.

Without ever expecting anything in return, Florence devoted her energy and time to shaping these young souls to become the best versions of themselves. Her ability to give, teach, and guide tirelessly has marked generations of young women. Still today, the imprint of her generosity is felt through those she helped, inspiring in turn those who knew her to follow her example. Florence is more than a mentor; she is a light for her community, illuminating the paths of those seeking to grow and prosper.

To fully honor the generosity and commitment of Florence Petit-Frère, an acrostic of her name reflects the deep values that drive her. Through each letter, we discover the strength of her character, her unwavering dedication, and the inspiration she offers to those fortunate enough to cross her path.

Acrostic for Florence Petit-Frère

Faithful in living out God's love and teachings.
Lifting others with her acts of generosity and care.
Open-hearted and always ready to help.
Radiating the light of Christ in her community.
Empowering others through her unwavering kindness.
Nurturing relationships with warmth and sincerity.
Courageously sowing seeds of hope and joy.
Elevating lives with her inspiring spirit.

Passionate about making a difference in others' lives.
Engaged in spreading the message of faith and love.
Tirelessly working to uplift her community.
Investing in people through her selfless actions.
Trusting in God's promises every step of the way.

Faithfully reflecting Christ's teachings in her deeds.
Resolute in promoting generosity and unity.
Encouraging others to embrace the power of giving.
Radiating kindness and compassion wherever she goes.
Elevating those around her with her dedication and grace.

Florence Petit-Frère is a model of dedication and selfless love. Her commitment to youth and her unwavering generosity continue to leave an indelible mark on the lives of those she supports. Her ability to give without expecting anything in return deeply inspires and makes her a beacon of light in her community.

MERLANDE DUVAL AUGUSTE

A RADIANT GENEROSITY

Merlande Duval Auguste is the perfect expression of generosity and dedication. From a young age, she always showed deep empathy toward others, but it is through her business that she has truly revealed the extent of her heart. She has dedicated her life to mentoring and supporting children and young people from disadvantaged backgrounds, offering them not only a future but also a sense of belonging and love.

What distinguishes Merlande is her ability to give without

ever expecting anything in return. Every smile she draws on the children's faces, every opportunity she creates, every word of encouragement she offers are gestures that deeply mark those who have the chance to cross her path. Her generosity inspires not only gratitude but also a willingness in others to follow her example.

She strongly reminds us that true wealth lies in sharing and that, through our actions, we have the power to transform the world around us.

After exploring the multiple facets of Merlande Duval Auguste's generosity, it becomes evident that her name itself embodies the grandeur of her actions. To grasp the very essence of her kindness, each letter of her first name reveals a unique quality, an aspect of her personality that reflects the profound impact she leaves on those around her. Let's discover together what each letter of her name hides, as many symbols of her exceptional dedication.

Acrostic for Merlande Duval Auguste:

Mission-driven, always seeking to uplift others.
Energized by faith, showing unwavering kindness.
Representing God's love with every gesture.
Lighting up lives with her generosity.
Acting with humility, inspiring transformation.
Never hesitant to share her blessings.
Dedicated to serving with a joyful heart.
Elevating others through acts of compassion.

Deeply rooted in her spiritual calling.
Uplifting lives with boundless love.
Vibrant in her faith, always giving more.
Always spreading joy through her actions.
Living as a true example of divine generosity.

Ambassador of hope in every encounter.
Uniting hearts with her unwavering commitment.
Glorifying God through every act of kindness.
Understanding the power of love in action.
Sowing seeds of transformation wherever she goes.
Trusting God in every mission she undertakes.
Eternally remembered for her generous spirit.

Merlande Duval Auguste, through her empathy and commitment, is a quiet force of generosity. Her immense heart, ready to give tirelessly, has transformed the lives of those she has supported. Merlande embodies the beauty of sharing, listening, and selfless love, a shining example for all.

LYNDA DUVAL

A GENEROUS HEART IN SERVICE OF OTHERS

Lynda Duval is a remarkable woman whose generosity knows no bounds. A loving and devoted cousin, she played a key role in the celebration of my 52nd birthday. She not only coordinated all the activities but also gave her time, energy, and resources with rare selflessness. Every detail of this special day bore her touch, and although she couldn't attend, her involvement was shining proof of her love and devotion.

What makes Lynda so inspiring is her ability to give without ever expecting anything in return. Her strength of character and boundless energy are at the service of those in need, and she always does it with a smile. She is a living example of what it truly means to "serve others" with love and kindness. Everyone who meets her can only be touched by her generosity and her deep desire to make every moment more beautiful, more radiant.

As we pause to reflect on the impact of people like Lynda, it is clear that her life embodies a profound lesson in generosity. Each letter of her name tells a story, a quality that reveals her essence. Let's discover together what her name inspires in us.

Acrostic of Lynda Duval:

Lifting others with her unshakable kindness.
Yearning to create a better world through giving.
Nurturing hope and faith in every life she touches.
Dedicated to serving with love and compassion.
Acting as a beacon of light in her community.

Deeply committed to spreading joy and peace.
Understanding the transformative power of generosity.
Valued for her unwavering faith and service.
Always walking in grace and humility.
Leaving a legacy of love for future generations.

May this tribute be a reflection of Lynda Duval's greatness of heart, and an invitation for us all to follow her example, to give with the same love and generosity.

MARLYSE LOUIDOR

A HEART THAT GIVES WITHOUT COUNTING

Marlyse Louidor is the embodiment of genuine generosity, the kind that expects nothing in return. Her immense heart and her ability to see beyond the immediate needs of others set her apart. During our graduation in hemodialysis in the United States, Marlyse showed rare attention and sensitivity. While I was in a difficult situation, unable to organize my own celebration, she invited me to her party, opening not only her home but also her heart with disarming simplicity.

This gesture, although simple in appearance, marked my

life. It reflects a generosity that goes beyond material goods to touch the very essence of friendship and support. Marlyse has this unique gift of always thinking of others before herself, of sowing joy and solidarity wherever she goes. Her way of giving, with heart, inspires all who meet her to embrace the same attitude of kindness. By her example, she reminds us that true wealth is found in acts of support and sharing.

Her name, Marlyse, in itself reveals the beauty of her qualities and the profound impact she leaves in our lives.

Let's discover together what each letter of her name reveals about her:

Making the world brighter with her generous heart.
Acting with humility, inspiring transformation.
Radiating kindness in every gesture.
Loving others unconditionally, as Christ taught.
Yearning to make an eternal impact through service.
Sharing blessings abundantly, touching countless lives.
Elevating others through her unwavering faith.

Living as a testimony of God's abundant love.
Opening her heart to those in need.
Uplifting spirits with her joyful presence.
Inspiring others to embrace acts of kindness.
Dedicating herself to creating a legacy of hope.
Overcoming challenges with steadfast determination.
Reflecting God's grace in every step of her journey.

Thus, Marlyse Louidor remains a figure of kindness and generosity, inspiring everyone to spread acts of love and solidarity around them.

LUCNAIRE DUVAL

A MODEL OF INSPIRING GENEROSITY AND LEADERSHIP

Lucnaire Duval is much more than an entrepreneur and a chartered accountant; he is a pillar in his community. Rather than boasting about his means, he puts his resources at the service of others, particularly in the social and educational fields. By choosing not to make money his master, but to put it at the service of those in need, Lucnaire embodies the spirit of generosity. He gives more than one would expect from him, acting humbly, and those closest to him affectionately call him Tchali, a sign of a well-deserved closeness and respect.

Through this commitment, Lucnaire leaves a lasting imprint in the hearts, and each letter of his name reflects a quality that inspires.

Let's discover together what each letter of "Lucnaire Duval" reveals and how they form a portrait of his exceptional impact:

Leading by example, a servant of God's will.
Upholding faith as the cornerstone of his life.
Committed to sowing seeds of generosity.
Nurturing others with wisdom and compassion.
Advocating for the power of faith in action.
Integrating love into every act of service.
Radiating peace and hope through his deeds.
Empowering communities with his generous spirit.

Dedicated to creating a better world for all.
Unshaken by challenges, anchored in faith.
Vibrant in his mission to inspire transformation.
Acting with courage, humility, and grace.
Leaving a legacy of hope and kindness.

Thus, Lucnaire Duval, through his altruism and inspiring leadership, constantly demonstrates that true wealth lies in what we share with others. He is a role model, a man whose very name evokes the values he embodies and spreads around him.

FELER EXALANT

A BEACON OF GENEROSITY FOR HIS COMMUNITY

Feler Exalant was a person deeply attached to his hometown, Limbé. From a young age, he knew how to invest his energy and passion for the wellbeing of his community, organizing football championships to allow teenagers to enjoy healthy entertainment and develop a team spirit. Always ready to help others, he was among the first to offer his support during the celebration of my birthday, bringing an unmatched energy, strength, and unwavering dedication.

Upon my arrival in the United States, Feler was the first to visit me, not only in person but also by supporting me financially, a testament to his deep generosity and sincere friendship. Although he did not have the opportunity to read this book, having left this world before its publication, his name deserves to be etched among those of the generous people of his generation.

To better honor this exceptional man, each letter of his first name reveals an aspect of his personality and commitment. Let's discover together what each letter of his name expresses about his unique legacy:

Faithfully serving as a reflection of God's love.
Elevating others through acts of kindness.
Lighting the path for those in need.
Enduring challenges with unshakable faith.
Resolute in spreading hope and joy.

Ever present as a source of strength for others.
Xemplifying generosity in every action.
Acting with humility and compassion.
Leading with love, inspiring transformation.
Always sowing seeds of hope and change.
Nurturing relationships that reflect God's grace.
Trusting in God's promises, unwavering in purpose.

Feler Exalant remains etched in our memories as a generous, authentic being deeply attached to his own. His legacy of kindness and dedication towards others inspires and continues to shine far beyond his physical presence. May his example drive us to embrace the same generosity and also sow in the lives of others.

REBECCA DEROCHE

A MODEL OF GENEROSITY AND MATURITY

Rebecca is a person whose generosity illuminates every place she touches. Met through Pastor Ernest Jean, I was immediately impressed by her exceptional maturity and her ability to give without expecting anything in return. During the Thanksgiving ceremony, Rebecca not only participated enthusiastically but she added a special touch to the decoration, making this event unique and unforgettable.

Her personal investment is a reflection of an open heart, ready to commit to others. Through simple gestures, she has shown that generosity is not only in great actions but in the details that transform an experience. Rebecca inspires those around her to follow her example, reminding them that each act of kindness, however humble, can have a profound and lasting impact. Her dedication is a living testimony of the power of a generous spirit.

Rebecca, through her kindness and commitment, embodies a form of generosity that goes beyond simple gestures. Every act she performs reflects constant concern for the well-being of others, and her impact on those around her is undeniable.

Through her name, we discover the profound qualities that define her and that inspire all those who have the chance to cross her path. Here is what each letter of her name reveals, a subtle portrait of her generosity:

Radiating kindness and grace in every moment.
Empowering others through her acts of generosity.
Beautifully embodying the spirit of giving.
Elevating lives with her unwavering faith.
Committed to creating a world filled with love.
Caring deeply for the well-being of others.
Advocating for hope and transformation.

Dedicating herself to God's divine mission.
Empowered by faith to serve selflessly.
Reaching hearts with her compassion.
Open-hearted in sharing her blessings.
Courageously standing as a light in dark times.
Hopeful in every step of her journey.
Eternal in her impact on those she meets.

Rebecca is a woman whose maturity and generosity leave a lasting impression. Her kindness, selfless actions, and sincere commitment show that true greatness lies in the small attentions that change lives. She embodies kindness and faith in action, always ready to sow to reap fruits of kindness around her.

RACHELLE DESROULEAUX

A SYMBOL OF INSPIRING GENEROSITY

Rachelle Desrouleaux embodies generosity in all its splendor. From her high school years in Haiti to our reunions in the United States, she has never stopped sowing kindness into the lives of those around her. Her ability to give without expecting anything in return, whether it be her time, listening, or support, makes her a role model to follow.

Rachelle has not only inspired through her actions, but she has also shown that generosity can touch and transform lives. Through her dedication, she has proven that sowing into the lives of others, with love and faith, always yields abundant fruits. She, in turn, inspires all those who have had the privilege of crossing her path to follow this path of kindness.

Rachelle Desrouleaux, through her gentleness and altruism, illuminates every moment shared with those she touches. Her generosity, far more than just a simple quality, is a force that transforms lives. She embodies kindness in every gesture, every word, and every commitment, showing us that true generosity is not measured by the size of actions but by the impact they leave on the hearts of others.

Let us now explore what each letter of her name reveals, a symbol of everything she represents and the inspiration she offers to those who know her.

Acrostic of Rachelle Desrouleaux:

Resolute in her mission to uplift others.
Acting with grace and unwavering faith.
Carrying hope into every corner of her life.
Helping others find peace and joy.
Elevating lives through her generous spirit.
Loving unconditionally, as God commands.
Living as an example of kindness and humility.
Empowering others with her acts of service.

Dedicated to making the world a better place.
Encouraging others to embrace generosity.
Sharing her blessings with open hands.
Reflecting God's love in every action.
Outstanding in her commitment to faith.
Uplifting hearts through her selfless deeds.
Lighting the way for those in need.

Endlessly inspired by God's grace.
Advocating for hope and transformation.
Uniting communities through her acts of love.
Xemplifying the true meaning of generosity.

Rachelle Desrouleaux is an inexhaustible source of generosity. Her actions, marked by kindness and love, remind us that every act of kindness, no matter how modest, can have a profound and lasting impact. She inspires everyone to follow this path of kindness and to show the same compassion towards others.

PAUL EMILE FRAZIL

A MODEL OF BOUNDLESS GENEROSITY

Paul Emile Frazil is the very embodiment of generosity. His immense heart and his ability to give without ever expecting anything in return make him a true role model for all who know him. When my son was having trouble adapting to school in Haiti, Paul welcomed him to the United States with touching kindness, treating him as if he were his own child.

This act, far from being isolated, reflects his deep commitment to others. Always ready to offer his help, Paul inspires with his altruism, availability, and sense of sacrifice. He shows that generosity lies not only in what we give materially but in the way we welcome and support others in difficult times. Thanks to his example, Paul Emile Frazil reminds us that true greatness lies in the selfless love we have for our fellow man.

Paul Emile Frazil, with his immense heart and unwavering altruism, has deeply touched those who crossed his path. There are no limits to his generosity, whether in the welcome, listening, or support he offers to those in need. Through his actions, Paul shows us that kindness and dedication can transform lives.

Now, let us discover through each letter of his first name the qualities that make him an inspiring model.

Acrostic:

Persevering in his mission to inspire others.
Acting with unwavering kindness and faith.
Uplifting hearts through acts of service.
Living as an example of Christ's love.

Elevating others with his dedication to generosity.
Making every action reflect God's grace.
Inspiring transformation through his compassion.
Leading with integrity and purpose.
Empowered by his faith to sow seeds of hope.

Faithfully walking in alignment with God's plan.
Radiating love through selfless giving.
Advocating for unity and spiritual growth.
Zealous in his commitment to inspire change.
Illuminating lives through his generosity.
Leaving a legacy of hope and encouragement.

In short, Paul Emile Frazil fully embodies the spirit of generosity and compassion. His actions, always imbued with kindness and altruism, testify to his deep humanity. Through his commitment and ability to reach out to those in need, he reminds us of the importance of sowing kindness around us. His example is a true source of inspiration, inviting us to reflect on our own impact on the world and on others.

ABDAHAM MONCOEUR

A MODEL OF GENEROSITY AND ALTRUISM

Abdaham Moncoeur is much more than an entrepreneur and a professor. He is a man of science, endowed with a rare empathy, who shows a deep commitment to those who need it most. His ability to combine intellectual rigor and generosity makes him an inspiring example. Always ready to respond to calls for help, Abdaham never hesitates to make himself available to support the less fortunate.

In critical moments, whether during humanitarian crises or simple situations of distress, Abdaham demonstrates exemplary dedication. His generosity knows no bounds, and he never counts what he gives, whether in time, resources, or energy. He inspires those around him to give without expecting anything in return, to cultivate kindness, and to surpass themselves to help their fellow human. Through his actions, he embodies altruism and leaves an indelible mark on the hearts of those he touches.

To illustrate the profound impact and generosity of Abdaham Moncoeur, it is essential to discover what each letter of his first name reveals about his personality. Each word, inspired by his qualities, testifies to his dedication and the altruism he embodies daily. The following acrostic highlights the distinctive traits of a man whose greatness of spirit inspires and motivates those who cross his path:

Always living to reflect God's love and compassion.
Building bridges of hope through kindness.
Demonstrating the power of faith in action.
Advancing the cause of generosity with humility.
Helping others grow spiritually and emotionally.
Acting as a light in moments of darkness.
Making every step count in his mission to serve.

Modeling Christ-like behavior in his daily life.
Open to the needs of others, always ready to give.
Never hesitating to share his blessings.
Courageously leading with faith and integrity.
Offering love and care to everyone he meets.
Endlessly dedicated to sowing seeds of hope.
Uplifting communities through his acts of service.
Reflecting God's abundant grace in all he does.

This acrostic reveals to what extent Abdaham Moncoeur is a model of generosity and altruism. Through his tireless dedication and unwavering commitment, he shows that a single individual can have a considerable impact on the world around him. Abdaham is a source of inspiration, reminding everyone that love for others and selfless action are the true pillars of a fulfilled life.

DAVID DORSAINVIL

A PILLAR OF GENEROSITY AND SERVICE

David Dorsainvil embodies generosity in all its splendor. A former football player, he successfully transferred the energy of his sports career to an even nobler mission: that of serving his community with dedication. Through his involvement with Radio Lumière, he has touched the lives of many people, especially young people, to whom he has offered guidance and support. Now living in Canada, David continues to tirelessly devote himself to altruistic acts, giving his time, skills, and resources without ever expecting anything in return.

Whether through his advice, prayers, or concrete actions, he inspires others to demonstrate the same generosity and to contribute to the well-being of their fellow man. His impact is felt far beyond borders, reminding us that the spirit of service is a force that transforms lives and inspires generations.

David Dorsainvil's generosity does not stop at his visible actions; it is present in every interaction, every act of love and kindness he displays daily. From his sports commitments to his crucial role at Radio Lumière, he has made his life a living testament to service and altruism. Every time David reaches out, he seeks nothing in return but gives with his heart.

It is this devotion to others that makes him so inspiring and invites everyone to discover the depth of his name, where each letter illustrates the qualities that define him. Let's discover together what each letter of his first name reveals about this exceptional man:

Dedicated to serving others with unwavering kindness,
Aspiring to spread hope and faith in every step,
Voice of encouragement to the weary and lost,
Inspired by divine love and truth,
Determined to make a lasting impact.

Driven by generosity that touches hearts,
Open-handed in both spirit and deeds,
Reflecting God's grace in every action,
Steadfast in faith, no matter the storm,
Advancing peace and unity wherever he goes,
Illuminating the path of others through compassion,
Nurturing relationships with integrity and care,
Victorious in sowing seeds of goodness,

Imprinted with the purpose to inspire,
Living each day as a testimony of love.

David Dorsainvil is a true model of generosity and service. His actions, driven by kindness and love, leave a lasting mark on the hearts of those he touches. Through his presence, he reminds us that generosity knows no borders and that each person, in their own way, can contribute to making the world a better place. His example inspires us to go beyond ourselves to serve others with faith and humility.

CONSTANCE LEVASSEUR

A LIFE OF MUSICAL GENEROSITY

At 92 years old, Constance Levasseur is a true icon of generosity. Throughout her life, she has used her exceptional talent as a musician and composer to touch hearts and enrich souls. What sets her apart is not just the longevity of her career, but her ability to give without expecting anything in return, offering her art as a source of comfort and inspiration.

Her commitment to the show "Morning Serum" is the most brilliant proof of this. Constance, despite her age, continues to contribute with passion and dedication. She embodies generosity in its purest form: one that inspires, elevates, and shows that true selflessness is a light that never goes out. Constance Levasseur is a role model for everyone, proving that at any age, one can transform others' lives through the generosity of spirit and the beauty of mind.

The greatness of Constance Levasseur lies in her ability to illuminate others with her music and unconditional love. Her journey is a symphony of generosity, where every note she has played resonates as a tribute to life and mutual aid. Despite the passing years, Constance remains an inexhaustible source of wisdom and kindness, proving that generosity knows no age or limits.

Let us discover through the letters of her name what makes her so unique, a true light in the lives of so many people:

Committed to spreading God's message of love.
Opening her heart to serve those in need.
Never withholding her blessings from others.
Sharing the light of faith wherever she goes.
Trusting in God's promises with steadfastness.
Advocating for hope and unity among her peers.
Nurturing others with her wisdom and care.
Courageously reflecting God's grace through action.
Endlessly inspired by Christ's example.

Living as a testimony of God's abundant love.
Empowering others through her acts of kindness.
Valuing every opportunity to sow seeds of generosity.
Advancing her mission of faith with dedication.
Shining brightly as a beacon of hope.
Supporting others with unwavering love.

Elevating lives with her thoughtful guidance.
Upholding the values of compassion and faith.
Reflecting Christ in her words and deeds.

Constance Levasseur is much more than a talented musician and composer; she is an unwavering force of generosity. Through every gesture, every note, she has left a lasting mark on the hearts of those she touched. Her example is an invitation to live with kindness, to give without counting, and to believe in the power of selflessness to transform the world.

MARIE-CARMELLE JEAN VERNET

A MODEL OF GENEROSITY AND FAITH

Marie-Carmelle Jean-Vernet is a woman whose generosity surpasses words. Her faithful presence and unwavering support are tangible proofs of her big heart. Throughout the writing of this book, she was always there, providing not only her help but also her inspiration. During the organization of my Thanksgiving ceremony, Carmelle once again stood out through her selfless commitment and love of service.

What makes Carmelle so special is her ability to give without ever expecting anything in return. Her sincere devotion, fueled by an unshakeable faith in God, illuminates the lives of those who have the privilege of knowing her. She is a living example of what it truly means to be at the service of others, inspiring those around her to follow her example of generosity and unconditional love.

Marie-Carmelle Jean Vernet is a woman whose imprint of generosity and faith deeply inspires those who know her. Each of her actions reflects her dedication to serving without expecting anything in return, a mark of her great soul. Her unwavering support and comforting presence illuminate the lives of many people, and her faith in God remains the source of her selfless commitment.

To better understand the essence of this exceptional woman, let's delve into each letter of her name, revealing the qualities that make her so special:

Motivated by her faith to uplift others.
Advocating for kindness and unity.
Radiating love in every interaction.
Inspiring others through her acts of service.
Elevating communities with her compassion.

Carrying hope into every corner of her life.
Always giving with a generous heart.
Resolute in spreading God's message of love.
Making every moment count in her mission to serve.
Empowering others to embrace acts of kindness.
Leaving a legacy of faith and generosity.
Living as an example of Christ's teaching.
Endlessly inspired by the spirit of giving.

Joyfully sharing her blessings with those in need.
Elevating lives through her dedication to service.
Advocating for hope and spiritual transformation.
Never hesitating to sow seeds of kindness.

Valuing the power of faith in action.
Empowered by God's grace to create change.
Reflecting Christ in every act of generosity.
Nurturing hearts and minds with her kindness.
Elevating others through her inspiring leadership.
Trusting in God's promises with steadfast faith.

Marie-Carmelle Jean Vernet is a beacon of generosity, an inexhaustible source of faith and devotion. Her life is a testimony of what it truly means to give without counting, inspiring those around her to follow this path of light and unconditional love. Through her presence, she transforms lives, offering an example of living faith and sincere service.

FRANCK ALFRÉNA

A GENEROUS AND DISCREET HEART

Franck Alfréna is the very embodiment of discreet yet infinitely precious generosity. In a period of my life when challenges seemed insurmountable, Franck intervened with exemplary kindness. Without ever seeking recognition, he facilitated my journey to the United States and opened the doors of his home to me, offering not only shelter but also constant moral support.

His altruism, although often unnoticed, has a lasting impact on all who have the chance to meet him. He gives with his heart, never expecting anything in return. Franck inspires with his humility and his ability to help, showing that true generosity lies in simple but sincere gestures. It is this discreet generosity that makes him a model of inspiration for all who surround him.

Franck Alfréna's generosity is not manifested through grand flamboyant gestures but rather in everyday actions imbued with kindness and sincerity. At every moment, he is there, present for those in need, never seeking the spotlight. Franck embodies a generosity that warms the heart, an unconditional support that soothes and accompanies. His impact, though discreet, is immense and leaves a lasting mark on the lives of those who have the privilege of knowing him.

To pay tribute to this extraordinary person, let's discover what each letter of his first name reveals about him:

Faithfully serving as a reflection of God's will.
Radiating love and hope through his deeds.
Advocating for unity and spiritual growth.
Never ceasing to inspire others through generosity.
Courageously stepping forward to make a difference.
Kind-hearted and devoted to acts of kindness.

Acting with grace and humility in every situation.
Lifting spirits with his unwavering compassion.
Focusing on God's purpose in his life.
Reflecting the light of Christ in all he does.
Élevating the lives of those he serves.
Nurturing others with his words and actions.
Advancing his mission of faith with dedication.

Franck Alfréna, with his generous heart and discretion, is a living example of what it truly means to give to others. His humility and unconditional support do not make noise, but they transform lives. It is in simple and sincere gestures that his greatness lies, and his impact, although invisible to many, is profound and lasting. He inspires to be better, simply by the example of his existence.

JACQUES JEAN-VERNET

A GENEROUS-HEARTED INTELLECTUAL

Jacques Jean-Vernet is much more than a professor, he is a true beacon for the Haitian youth. Passionate about social and political issues, he continuously puts his expertise at the service of others, especially the young students he mentors with kindness. His generosity translates into a constant commitment to train and support those who aspire to build a better future for their country.

Endowed with great discretion, Jacques shares his knowledge without expecting anything in return, animating each discussion with a profound desire to advance his community. His methodological support has enabled many students to succeed thus, marking their academic journey in a lasting way. His dedication and humility make him an inspiring model, reminding us that true generosity lies in the art of giving with heart and knowledge.

Through his actions, Jacques Jean-Vernet embodies a model of service and dedication that deeply affects those who have the chance to be around him. His ability to share his knowledge, to enlighten young minds, and to demonstrate a silent but constant generosity testifies to his greatness of soul. Each of his contributions is a step towards a better future for others, particularly for the Haitian youth whom he inspires with his commitment and kindness.

To fully grasp the essence of this exceptional person, let's discover together what each letter of his name reveals:

Joyfully reflecting God's love in his daily life.
Advocating for kindness and selflessness.
Courageously stepping forward to inspire change.
Quietly serving with humility and grace.
Uplifting lives through acts of generosity.
Elevating others with his unwavering faith.
Shining as a beacon of hope and compassion.

Journeying through life as a faithful servant of God.
Engaging communities with his acts of kindness.
Always trusting in God's promises.
Nurturing relationships with care and dedication.

Valuing the transformative power of giving.
Exemplifying Christ's teachings in every act.
Resolute in spreading God's message of hope.
Never hesitating to share his blessings.
Empowering others to live with purpose and faith.
Tirelessly sowing seeds of generosity and love.

Jacques Jean-Vernet is much more than an intellectual, he is a living example of how knowledge, when shared with kindness and generosity, can transform lives. His impact on youth and his community goes beyond words, and it is in his discrete but profoundly significant acts that his true greatness lies. A model of humility and service, Jacques continues to inspire through his life dedicated to others.

LYTTON LEGROS

AN AMBASSADOR OF GENEROSITY AND SOLIDARITY

Lytton Legros is much more than a former athlete; he is a man of heart. A former football player for the prestigious Victory Sportif Club, he has turned his passion into a true commitment to the well-being of others. Beyond the fields, Lytton has dedicated his life to helping those in need, embodying genuine and selfless generosity.

An active member of the Association of Former Limbé Football Players, he never hesitates to step in, whether it is to support a friend in trouble or to answer the call of a greater cause. Always ready to lend a hand, Lytton is an example of altruism for everyone fortunate enough to know him. Through his constant commitment, he embodies solidarity, proving that generosity can change lives and inspire generations.

Lytton Legros, through his dedication and kindness, embodies a model of generosity that is not just about words, but manifests through concrete actions. His ability to turn every situation into an opportunity to lend a hand, support, and comfort makes him an ambassador of solidarity. What is remarkable about Lytton is that every gesture, no matter how humble, has a profound impact on those who cross his path.

Let's now discover what each letter of his first name reveals about the very essence of this extraordinary man:

Living a life dedicated to uplifting others.
Yielding to God's will with unwavering faith.
Trusting in the power of kindness and hope.
Thoughtfully guiding others toward their purpose.
Open-hearted and ready to serve.
Never ceasing to inspire those around him.

Leading by example through acts of generosity.
Elevating lives with his encouraging spirit.
Giving selflessly to strengthen his community.
Reflecting God's light in every step he takes.
Overcoming challenges with faith and determination.
Shining as a symbol of love and service.

Lytton Legros is not just a former athlete but a true pillar of the community. His unwavering commitment to others, his generosity, and his ability to build bridges between generations make him a model of altruism and humanity. Whether on the field or in his daily life, Lytton continues to inspire with his dedication and deep desire to change lives, reminding everyone of the importance of solidarity.

GUERDA PIERRE

A LIFE OF GENEROSITY AND FAITH

Guerda Pierre is an exceptional woman, a true embodiment of generosity and faith. A singer devoted to the glory of God, she uses her talent to inspire and uplift the souls of those who listen to her. But her generosity is not limited to her artistic gifts: she is always ready to offer her time and energy to support others, even when she lacks material means.

During the Thanksgiving ceremony organized for my birthday, Guerda showed immense generosity, contributing to the success of the event through her dedication and talent. Her example inspires everyone who knows her to give without expecting anything in return, showing that love and service are the greatest gifts one can offer. Her ability to encourage others to achieve great feats through her singing and support is a model for all.

This generosity and unwavering faith that reside in Guerda are not only reflected in her words but also in each of her actions. She embodies a rare model of altruism and dedication, touching the lives of all who cross her path. Through her talent, she conveys hope, and through her heart, she offers sincere and deep love. Guerda reminds us that true self-giving does not lie in the quantity of what one possesses, but in the quality of what one shares.

The acrostic of her name reveals even more the hidden treasures of this inspiring woman.

Giving with an open heart and boundless generosity.
Uplifting others with her acts of kindness.
Empowering her community through faith and love.
Resolutely serving as an example of Christ's teachings.
Demonstrating compassion in every situation.
Advocating for unity and spiritual growth.

Passionate about spreading God's love.
Inspiring others through her unwavering faith.
Elevating lives by sowing seeds of hope.
Reflecting God's grace in all she does.
Reminding others of the power of generosity.
Endlessly dedicated to serving her community.

Guerda, through her voice, actions, and love, illuminates the path of those around her. She inspires both through her humility and her ability to give without expecting anything. Her life is a vibrant testament to what it means to live for others, and her legacy of generosity will continue to inspire all those who have the chance to know her.

SALINA CHARLES

AN ARTISTIC GENEROSITY WITHOUT LIMITS

Salina Charles is a woman whose generosity shines through music. From a young age, when she was ranked among the top artists at the prestigious "Chanter Noël" competition in Haiti in 1999, she has never ceased to impress with her talent and passion. What makes Salina truly special is her deep desire to share this gift with others, never expecting anything in return.

Now well-established in the United States, she continues

to bring comfort and joy to the Haitian community through her songs. Her voice, both gentle and powerful, transcends boundaries and touches hearts. Salina does not use her talent solely for her own glory but puts it at the service of those in need of comfort, transforming ordinary moments into moments of grace.

I have been immensely privileged to benefit from her unwavering generosity. On every occasion, she gives not only her time and talent but also her heart. Salina inspires those around her to be more generous, reminding us that the act of giving, be it a smile, a song, or a word of support, has the power to transform lives.

Acrostic: Salina Charles

Shining brightly as a beacon of hope and faith.
Acting with humility and compassion toward others.
Loving unconditionally as a reflection of Christ's love.
Inspiring others to embrace the spirit of giving.
Nurturing relationships through selfless acts.
Advancing God's mission with unwavering dedication.

Carrying the light of faith wherever she goes.
Helping others grow spiritually and emotionally.
Always giving with a cheerful and generous heart.
Radiating kindness and inspiring transformation.
Lifting spirits with her words and deeds.
Elevating lives by embodying the values of Christ.
Spreading joy and hope through her faith and actions.

In conclusion, Salina Charles perfectly embodies generosity through art. Her music is an inexhaustible source of comfort and hope. She teaches us that true greatness lies not only in talent but in how one uses that talent to elevate and transform the lives of others.

JOSEPH PATRICK

A MAN OF HEART AND ACTION

Joseph Patrick embodies the essence of genuine generosity. Passionate about football from a young age, he founded the club "Canal Plus" in Limbe, offering much more than just a training space. For him, every meeting on the field is an opportunity to guide young people, not only in physical effort but also in their personal development. Gifted with a natural talent for motivating and encouraging, Joseph has always used his abilities to serve others.

What distinguishes Patrick is his unwavering altruism.

Driven by a deep sense of sharing and selflessness, he willingly sacrifices his own opportunities to help others move forward. In his journey, he has given up several "golden opportunities" that could have changed his life, preferring to dedicate himself to the collective well-being. His generosity inspires and touches all those who have the chance to be around him, encouraging them to follow his example.

To honor this generosity, let's discover what each letter of his name, Patrick Joseph, reveals about him.

Acrostic: Joseph Patrick

Journeying through life as a faithful steward of God.
Open to the needs of those around him.
Sharing his blessings with love and humility.
Elevating others through acts of kindness.
Proclaiming God's word through his deeds.
Helping to build a stronger, more compassionate community.

Passionate about spreading hope and faith.
Advocating for generosity as a way of life.
Trusting in God's provision and promises.
Reflecting Christ's teachings in every interaction.
Investing in the lives of others through selfless giving.
Carrying out God's mission with steadfast devotion.
Kind-hearted and ready to serve whenever needed.

Joseph Patrick is a model of dedication and kindness, a true pillar for his community. His mark is characterized by acts of generosity that exceed expectations, deeply touching those around him. Through his actions, he reminds us that true wealth lies in what we share with others, and he encourages everyone to pursue this path of generosity.

MARIE FRANCE SAINT-FLEURY

A CULINARY GENEROSITY IN THE SERVICE OF OTHERS

Marie France Saint-Fleury embodies generosity in its most exquisite form. From the moment I arrived in the United States, she was the first to warmly welcome me, offering a carefully prepared dish to welcome me. This gesture was just the beginning of a long series of acts of kindness that illustrate her open heart and constant willingness to help others.

A respected chef, Marie France uses her culinary talents not only to nourish bodies but also to comfort souls. She cooks not just with ingredients but with love and attention, transforming each meal into an experience of sharing and union. Her culinary art becomes a bridge between hearts, a vector of generosity that touches everyone fortunate enough to taste her dishes.

Always ready to help when called upon, Marie France never does things halfway. Whether supporting a cause, helping a neighbor, or offering a comforting smile, she does it with admirable modesty, never expecting anything in return. Her impact on those around her is immense, inspiring everyone to adopt the same generosity and find simple but powerful ways to make a difference.

This ability to give with so much heart is reflected in every aspect of her life, and each letter of her name seems to reveal a unique aspect of her generous personality. Let's now discover what each letter of "Marie France Saint-Fleury" inspires us.

Acrostic: Marie France Saint-Fleury

Moving through life as a vessel of God's love.
Advancing the cause of faith and generosity.
Radiating kindness and compassion to all.
Investing in others through acts of selflessness.
Elevating her community with grace and humility.

Faithfully walking in alignment with God's purpose.
Reflecting the light of Christ in her daily life.
Advocating for hope and spiritual growth.
Nurturing relationships with care and intention.
Courageously spreading joy and positivity.
Embodying the values of service and compassion.

Shining as a beacon of hope and faith.
Acting with purpose and dedication to God's work.
Inspiring others to embrace the power of giving.
Never hesitating to share her blessings with others.
Tirelessly sowing seeds of love and faith.

Focusing on God's mission with determination.
Lifting others with her unwavering kindness.
Empowering her community through acts of service.
Upholding Christ's teachings in all she does.
Reminding everyone of the beauty of generosity.
Yielding to God's will with steadfast faith.

In conclusion, Marie France Saint-Fleury is a true model of generosity. Through her simple yet profound actions, she reminds us that giving of oneself with love and sincerity is an act that transforms lives. Her example will remain etched in the hearts of those who have crossed her path.

CONCLUSION OF THE SECOND PART

The conclusion of this second part of *Sowing in the Lives of Others: A Generosity that Changes Destiny* reminds us that generosity is not just about simple gestures or material donations. It is a state of mind, an inner force that drives us to sow love, hope, and solidarity around us. Through the stories and portraits of these extraordinary individuals, we have discovered that every act of kindness, however humble, can have a profound and lasting impact on the lives of others.

These examples of generosity show us that it is possible to transform lives by simply being present, sharing our resources, our talents, and our time. Each of us can be a source of inspiration and change. May these testimonies encourage us to continue sowing without expecting in return, for this is how we contribute to the blossoming of a more humane, just, and bright world.

This gallery of generous souls is not an endpoint but an invitation to continue this work of generosity in our daily lives.

FINAL CONCLUSION

Throughout the pages of this book, we have traveled the path of generosity in its many forms, discovering its spiritual roots, its tangible benefits, and above all its profound impact on our lives and those of others. Generosity, as described here, is much more than a simple material gift or act of kindness: it is an inner transformation that changes the perception we have of the world and our role within it. It reflects the unconditional love of God, who calls us to share without expectations, to love without measure, and to sow without limits.

The stories, testimonies, and examples of lives dedicated to the service of others that we explored in the second part remind us that every action, no matter how small, can be a source of light and comfort for those who need it most. These inspiring figures show us that true generosity lies not only in grand acts, but in the consistency of small gestures that, day after day, shape a better world.

In conclusion, this book is not only an invitation to reflect on generosity but a call to action. May each of us, at our own level, sow seeds of kindness, solidarity, and love. For in giving, we do not only transform the lives of others, but we transform ourselves, becoming instruments of peace, justice, and light. May this work continue in our hearts and daily actions, so that generosity is not an exception, but indeed a way of life.

APPENDICES

LIST OF BIBLICAL REFERENCES

1. Proverbs 11:25

"A generous person will prosper; whoever refreshes others will be refreshed."

This verse reminds us that generosity, whether material or spiritual, brings blessings.

2. Corinthians 9:6-7

"Each of you should give what you have decided in your heart to give, not reluctantly or under compulsion, for God loves a cheerful giver." An invitation to give joyfully, without feeling compelled, but with faith and love.

3. Matthew 6:31-33

"But seek first his kingdom and his righteousness, and all these things will be given to you as well."

A reminder that God takes care of His children and generosity is a form of faith in His provision.

4. Exodus 35:5

"From what you have, take an offering for the Lord."

A divine instruction to bring offerings as a sign of obedience and devotion.

5. Luke 6:38

"Give, and it will be given to you. A good measure, pressed down, shaken together and running over, will be poured into your lap."

A principle of divine reciprocity in generosity.

References

The Gospel Coalition

Articles and reflections on biblical generosity and how to apply it in our Christian lives. evangile21.thegospelcoalition.org

Bible Gateway

A site where you can read Bible verses on generosity and discover how God blesses gifts given with faith.

biblegateway.com

Sources Chrétiennes

A site that offers theological commentary and patristic texts on biblical principles, including generosity.

sourceschretiennes.org

1. Bibliquest. (n.d.). Bible Verses by Subject. Retrieved from

https://www.bibliquest.net/Versets/Versets-Promesses_Bibliques.htm

2. Bible Gateway. (n.d.). Exodus 35:4-40:38 SG21

- Construction of the Tabernacle. Retrieved from https://www.biblegateway.com/passage/?search=Exode%2035%3A4-40%3A38&version=SG21

1. Gospel 21. (2019, May 6). 5 things that Exodus 25 teaches us about the offering. Retrieved from https://evangile21.thegospelcoalition.org/article/5-choses-apprend-exode-25-offrande/

2. Regine Translation. (n.d.). Translation of Chinese Proverbs (Expressions and Chengyu). Retrieved from http://www.regine-traduction.com/proverbes-chinois.php
3. Christian Sources. (n.d.). Home. Retrieved from https://sourceschretiennes.org/

PHOTOS OF THE THANKSGIVING CEREMONY

HAPPY

HAPPY
HAPPY
HAPPY

www.ingramcontent.com/pod-product-compliance
Lightning Source LLC
LaVergne TN
LVHW020018170826
845678LV00001B/36

* 9 7 9 8 8 9 6 9 1 1 2 4 1 *